Dorothy Sessa's

Thank You MLM

"Thank You MLM *by Dorothy Sessa is a moving and powerful story that tells us about the author's search to find love, happiness and meaning in her life. In the end she finds all three, but not where she expected to find them.*

Dorothy's journey has been full of hard work, self-examination and life experience. She struggled to start and run her own business hoping success and independence would bring her happiness. Her desire to be herself and to know herself has led her from feelings of worthlessness to feelings of jubilation. Relationships with family and friends have brought her great joy but also pain. Her story is shared with refreshing honesty and humour.

She shows us that God's unconditional love is for all of us - but to believe that, to accept it and to really love yourself is not easy. Holding God's love at the centre of your life and letting that love take control of your decisions and your relationships requires a lot of courage, but Dorothy believes that the rewards are awesome.

Thank you, Dorothy, for sharing your wonderful story and your passion for life with us and for 'espressing yourself' so well."

Bev Chambers
Retired ESL Program Manager

"Transitioning is not always trouble free but it is always achievable. There are moments that come and go in every individual's life when they feel that they have exerted all possible efforts. It is then that they may start to feel or desire the need of a transition whether it is something that will change their entire lifestyle or something to make their days run a little smoother. Happiness is the key in life; sometimes with a little help, contentment is the life-long outcome. I suggest and recommend Dorothy's book to anyone who wants to make a life-changing transition."

Lina Castle
Lina's Italian Market
Calgary, Alberta

"I have personally witnessed the changes and growth of Dorothy over these past years. Having known her from birth, I have seen her change from holding everything inside, being very quiet, to a person that is stepping outside her comfort zone and actively engaging in understanding herself and her relationships. Dorothy is a wonderful person, with a huge heart and truly wants to help others by sharing her experiences. Keep on your path, never stop growing - you go girl!"

Patti Lathrop

"Dorothy's path to personal awareness is one of immense possibility and of hope - hope her struggles will lead her to a higher level. Her personal journey through life is a struggle that everyone encounters but few have the humility to admit. Her progress was like a downpour of rain - full of love, discovery and learnings for all who were witness. Thank you Dorothy, for sharing."

Natalie Gibson, Marketing Specialist
President, InnoVisions and Associates
Airdrie, Alberta

"Dorothy's vulnerable openness is a refreshing expression of understanding one's road to self-discovery."

Dr. Susan Janssens, B.Sc. ND

Thank You MLM

Dorothy Sessa

Always & Forever Publishing   Amethyst Publishing

Calgary, Alberta

Distribution and ordering inquiries:
    Always & Forever Publishing
    #110, 919 Centre Street NW
    Calgary AB T2E 2P6
Order online at www.ThankYouMLM.com
To book Dorothy for speaking engagements, contact 1-877-304-6860

ISBN-10: 0-9780347-0-8

Book and cover design by Amethyst Publishing, Calgary, Alberta
Cup illustrations © Cheryl Peddie, 2007
Door mat © Ellen Edith, www.ellenedith.com
Author's photograph © PoGoPix Studios, 2006
Every effort has been made to contact the copyright owner of the poem
"Twenty Four Things to Remember" to obtain permission to reprint it
here.

Printed and bound in Canada

The Biggest Thank You Ever to Each and Every One of You

God for giving me a purpose to my life.

Vincenzo (man of my dreams) for your LOVE, financial support & encouragement for the book as well as putting up with me & my stuff!

Josephine, Melinda & Peter (gifts from God) for your emotional support, willingness & permission to share my story.

"ALL" my customers who supported me while I was a Multi-Level Marketer.

Craig & Alesia for introducing me to MLM.

Natalie for standing beside me as I learned to walk and talk the language of business.

Brenda for helping me put my first thoughts on paper.

Cathy for designing my websites.

Patricia M for suggesting the MLM theme.

Heather for educating me on the publishing industry.

Sheelagh for helping me get started & enlightening me with the perspective of Love.

Vanessa for doing such a great job at asking the right questions & making the message simple & clear for the reader.

Pat K for your first-class editing.

Anna-Mae for your valuable consulting & proof reading.

Ada for your gift of the coffee cups.

Cheryl for your talent at bringing my coffee cups to life.

Eileen for your detailed strategic business coaching.

Stéphanie for coaching & inviting me to change the way I looked at me & my life.

Dr. Susan Janssens for accepting my commitment to donate proceeds from my profits in support of your dream for the Maya Centre.

This story is dedicated to

My MLM friend, Terri, whom I loved and supported
through her transition in life.

My mom, Shirley, whom I failed to love and support
through her transition because
she didn't live up to my expectations.
Please forgive me, I really do love you Mom!

My inner child, Dorothy, whom I now love as you are.
I forgive you for failing to love yourself and others
while transitioning from worthless to priceless.

Contents

*"The average human
looks without seeing, listens without
hearing, touches without feeling, eats
without tasting, moves without physical
awareness, inhales without awareness
of odour or fragrance,
and talks without thinking."*

Leonardo da Vinci

Foreword

Just be yourself !
Dorothy ♡

Have you ever been inspired by love? I know you have. So you remember how it feels. *Thank You MLM* is my love story, or rather, lack of love story. It's the story of the dream I had of owning my own business. While on my journey with MLM (Multi-Level Marketing), I renewed my relationship with me, my God, and my family. In the end, MLM awakened me from an emotional coma, and enabled me to discover the secret to success in life: knowing who I **really wasn't**.

I met a lot of great people along the way. The one I remember the most is the **real me**.

Think about how you are in your life. Are you for real?

I hope that as you read my story, with all the faults, missteps, and challenges that came along with it, that you fall in love with you & your life, and that you will be inspired to be the **real you**, just as I was.

MLM is a non-traditional method of earning an income. You build your business by marketing to your loyal family and friends as customers – or even business partners. In a nutshell, the marketing strategy is to expand your business of customers and partners by networking with your family and friends. It's what some people call a pyramid scheme. But believe me, this was **a real business**; it was very hard work, and it forced me to take a close look at who I was.

When I was introduced to MLM, I created my own business formula:

Wife		
Mother	+ 3 kids x 23 years = **My Turn**	

Before MLM, I never thought of leaving my comfort zone, of taking a risk. Once I discovered MLM, though, I lost my comfort zone.

As I am fond of a good cup of espresso coffee, I like to call it "espressing" myself. MLM became my experiential education, and Mamma Mia, how I learned to espress-o myself!

I believe my experience with MLM was the **right business** at the **right time**. It was a direction God sent me to feel alive and to find the real me, although it wasn't the way out of silence, depression and unhappiness.

Thank You MLM is my story from the bottom of my heart, and from the bottom of my coffee cup.

> *Authentically me,*
>
> *Dorothy Sessa/Mamma D*
>
> *Encourager, Speaker, Author*

Chapter One

Multi-Level Magnetism

Have you been looking for Love?

I don't remember the moment I came into the world, but I do remember the moment my first sibling did. I remember thinking, "Now he's going to get all the attention, all the love. There's no more left for me. I guess I'll just have to earn my parents' love."

I was the best, the very best big sister in the world. I took care of my brother all the time. And then, not too long after he was born, there came a beautiful baby girl.

"Look at her! She's so beautiful, more beautiful than me. I'll just have to work harder to earn my parents' love."

Being the big sister was hard work. I was Mommy's little helper. I always came to the rescue. I had a lot of fun playing with my baby brother and sister. When it was time for me to go to school and leave them at home without me, I could hardly wait to come home for lunch to play with them again and help my mommy. Then it was off to the real world, school, for the afternoon, only to come home again to play and help. Helping, helping and helping some more: that's what I did to earn my parents' love. It was hard work earning love.

Many years went by, and another sibling came along, a beautiful bouncing baby boy. "That's okay. Look how beautiful he is! He'll love me, even if my parents don't. I'll take good care of him."

But as time went by, I got tired of being the big sister. I was tired of always helping and looking out for them. I started thinking about me, about how I could get more attention. But I didn't do anything about it. I simply waited.

When I started junior high school, I started noticing boys and liked the attention that I got from them. I fell in love for the first time, and I thought he had fallen in love with me. I thought we would get married and live happily ever after. But no. I remember that I was learning how to knit. I was knitting him a scarf, but he broke up with me before I finished it. That beautiful half-finished scarf ended up in the garbage.

Long after that shattered dream, I continued my search for love, carrying around my self-inflicted wounds. I wanted to start a family of my own. This family would deserve the love that I kept inside my heart, and would return it. It was all about me; I wanted to be loved, and give love in return. My desire was buried deep within me. I had been afraid to ask for some attention, afraid to ask for some time alone with my mom or dad. Somehow, growing up, I came to the conclusion that I was responsible for everyone's happiness. This meant that I had to be careful about what I said, but as I didn't really know how to be careful, I decided it was safer to just shut up. My love burned and grew in silence.

In my mid-teens, I entered the work world as a waitress at a local Italian restaurant. I had so much fun there. I got lots of attention, and I enjoyed serving others. I became good friends with the Italian mammas in the kitchen. Most of the kitchen staff was part of the same family. They welcomed me to be a part of their family, too.

In my twenties, I was at the cabaret every weekend, dancing, dancing and dancing some more. My cousin and I would go together. One night, while I was minding my own business, I watched a guy walk across the dance floor, heading towards our table. I remember thinking that I wouldn't mind getting to know him.

He walked, talked and dressed differently; he spoke

the romantic language of Love. This Italian-speaking young man had only been in Canada six months. I guess he wanted to get to know me, too, because he asked my cousin for my phone number. The rest is history.

This handsome young Italian immigrant, Vince, (short for Vincenzo) would soon be my husband. He represented my chance to be the best wife and mom ever. The burning desire that I had to get married, have children, and provide a stable and loving family environment, was a good fit with a man who wanted to settle down and start a family in his new home, Canada.

We married in November 1976 after dating for a year and a half. I became the happy housewife, and jumped into my marriage with both feet. I was always serving, as the way to my husband's heart was through his stomach. I cooked and I cooked and I cooked. I made it my mission to learn all the Italian traditions to please my husband, so that I would earn his love and never lose it. At the same time, I came to accept the love of Jesus Christ soon after the birth of our first child. What more could a woman ask for? I had a husband who loved me, a baby girl to love, and God's love. And then more love came into our home: another baby girl and then a son.

In our early days of marriage, I sometimes tried to give my opinion on a subject after listening to Vince's concerns. All I got was a louder husband. I had no idea love could be so loud! Fear began its journey into my heart and into my marriage. I became silent. (See page 239 for my warning signals.) My marriage had been my chance to break away from all those years of pleasing everyone else, of living up to everyone else's expectations. As unfair as it seemed, I soon learned that I was still required to play this role in order to keep peace around the house. A mountain of resentment began to build inside of me.

Unspoken, I began finding fault. At every opportunity I made Vince wrong, while in my own mind I was right. And while this habit made me feel better or smarter temporarily, little did I know that it was destroying my marriage. After twenty-three years with Vince and raising our family, listening to this loud voice of love, my "nobody loves me and I'm not good enough" story, the one I had so carefully crafted and nurtured, was on replay in my head.

This was a terrible time in my life, fraught with depression and feelings of worthlessness. I was 44 years old, with happy grown children, a wonderful husband and a beautiful home—yet it seemed my life was empty and meaningless. Vince loved his life. He owned his own business, played soccer, and was always making new friends. Whatever he did in life, he did passionately, and here I was feeling sorry for myself, wanting some of this passion for my life too.

Then, one day, I was introduced to an amazing new world, where people were supportive, enthusiastic and energetic. It was called MLM, short for multi-level marketing. It was just what the doctor ordered and I jumped in over my head. Not only did it give me a reason to get out of the house now that our children had grown up and started lives of their own, MLM presented a way for me to own my own business too.

But MLM represented much more than these things to me. I would finally be able to contribute to the family income after all the years of spending somebody else's hard-earned money.   It meant freedom. Having my own income would not only take some pressure off my hard-working and loyal husband, but having my own income would give me a say in what we did with our money! How could Vince refuse me if I wanted to spend **my** money on taking more trips together?

Most of all, MLM meant being surrounded by people who would support me in all that I did. MLM meant people would want to hear what I had to say.

But before they could, things had to change in our Christian family, headed by the Italian painter and his almost-Italian wife. Change, in more ways than one.

It happened quickly at Vince's job site. Vince and his work crew had just finished spraying the woodwork in the house and were preparing to go out for lunch. Suddenly, flames burst from a static spark, igniting two chemicals used to clean the spray machine. A five-gallon pail of lacquer and all the rags were close by. Vince tried to put the fire out, and suffered burns on his hands and lips as a result. They soon realized the fire was out of control, and called 9-1-1 as they fled the house. Once the fire was under control, the paramedics treated them for smoke inhalation, and then they were sent home.

Vince came home from work early that day with his face blackened by smoke and soot. I had no idea what had happened to him. Not seeing his anguish, I simply inquired as to what he had been spraying that was so dark. He told me about the fire. Shocked, I asked question after question, unable to comprehend how such a disaster could have happened.

Vince cleaned himself up, and we went back to the job site to assess the damage. There were a few windows broken and black soot on the exterior stucco where the smoke had escaped. Inside, all the woodwork in the house was burned, and there was black soot covering all of the drywall. The lid of the pail of lacquer had bubbled. Had the fire continued for just a few more minutes, the can might have exploded while the firemen were still in the house.

Vince and I stood on the site, traumatized. Yet, there was a lot to be thankful for; no one had been seriously injured and the house was still standing, thanks to the quick response time of the fire department. But reality began to set in as we sat in the car of the insurance adjuster, answering all his questions.

Years ago, I had suggested we get insurance coverage for the business, but Vince opposed the idea. As the years went by and no need came up, we never thought about insurance again. What damage could a painter do to a house? Maybe spill a can of paint on the carpet? We could handle that kind of expense. But in October 1999, we knew different. There we were, without any liability insurance coverage, and wondering how we'd pay for the fire's extensive damage.

Just before the fire, Vince and I had been upset with each other. We had had an argument over a paint colour on a job. The fire taught us many lessons, in business and in life. It seemed God was using this argument to show me how to get to the source of my feelings. God was teaching me to let go and move on. He wanted me to understand once and for all that the reason I was upset was not the reason I was upset.

I had a stronghold of resentment and anger in my heart that I was not ready to let go of. (See page 239 for my warning signals.) Not being able to look past my own pain, I left Vince to deal with the fire without my help. Thank goodness the builder stood by his side, supporting him from start to finish, telling him that one day in heaven they would laugh about the fire.

The aftermath of the fire was a difficult ordeal for Vince and the builder. The insurance company took a long time to finish their estimate, which came back at $90,000 in damages. To avert financial disaster, both Vince and the builder asked the insurance company to leave after the initial fire clean up so that they could deal with the restoration of the house. In doing so, Vince and the builder saved about half of what the insurance company was going to charge. Had the house burned down, we could have lost more than our life savings. That fire was a turning point in our lives, teaching us many lessons that weren't easy to learn.

I had been a stay-at-home mom for twenty-three years and had been on a pity party for some time, and even at this point in my life, my feelings of not being loved were returning. I was becoming accustomed to being alone while my family spent most of their time away from home. I felt unneeded and unloved as I went through many bouts of depression. Vince could not understand what was wrong with me. He kept saying, "There are women out there who would kiss my feet for the life I have given you!" I asked him to bring one of these women home. He never did.

Even though Vince and I were not getting along well, and there were still the after-effects of the fire to deal with, we decided to continue with our plan to celebrate our anniversary in Hawaii. We were enjoying a two-hour sunset cruise off the island of Maui when a lady approached me in the buffet line.

"Hello," she said. "You're the one from Canada?"

"Yes, I am," I replied.

"There's something exciting happening in Canada, and I'd like to talk to you about it later," she said.

The woman introduced herself as Alesia. She and her husband Craig were in Hawaii celebrating their anniversary as well. She promised to look for me when we got off the boat. I went back to our table and told Vince what had just happened. Her comments had sparked my interest. Yes! I wanted to be involved in something exciting for a change. With the fire being so fresh, realizing we could have lost more than our life savings, we thought this business opportunity would fit well.

Vince and I met with Alesia and Craig as we disembarked from the boat. Craig was also of Italian descent, so the men hit it off immediately. We walked and talked for an hour. Vince and I took their business card as we went our separate ways. As we parted, I promised to call them in a week. Seven days seemed such a long time to wait—Vince and I were going home the next day, but Alesia and Craig would not be home in Dallas until the following week.

Chapter Two

Multi-Level Meaning

What meaning do you give to life?

Finally, I made the call.

Alesia, my soon-to-be MLM sponsor, promised to find a meeting for me to attend so I could learn more about this business. It was December 7, 1999, when I went to the meeting that would change my life forever.

I immediately said yes to the opportunity. I wanted to have my own business and be involved in something BIG. I called Alesia to tell her that I had signed up. Congratulating me, Alesia asked, "Do you need any help?"

"No, I can do it by myself," I proclaimed.

"If you change your mind, let me know," she said.

I had been super mom, super volunteer, super woman, super friend, heck, I had done it all. I didn't need anybody's help. Me and God, we would pull this off.

Little did I realize that the secret to success in this business was 'asking for a favour,' which really meant asking for help. I would be asking my family and friends to be my customers, to support me in my new business.

I was considered a multi-level marketer. I even had a direct seller license. I went to a special training meeting two days later, featuring two trainers from out of town. Wow, I thought excitedly. Here I was, I was being trained for success by friendly, high-energy people: a friendly lady from Ontario and a young man from Detroit.

My elation soon wore off. Within minutes, they warned me that there was a lot of rejection in the MLM business. My heart sank. I found myself slouching in my chair. I started wondering what had I gotten myself into, and I could feel myself slipping back into that state of hopelessness I had briefly escaped.

But when I felt that, I found strength. Or desperation. Enough was enough. I had to fight this thing called depression. Then I remembered a moment only a year before, after working in a coffee shop for three short months. I had walked away from that job with the realization that I did not enjoy working for someone else. Vince, however, was not willing to borrow $300,000 for a franchise! At that point, I had called upon my God to show me what to do with the rest of my life. And in His time, he had brought me here. I sat up straight in my chair and said to myself, Let's do it anyway!

They taught me many things that day. Primarily, I learned that when you got your family and friends to support you in the business, and if you maintained their support, you eventually got paid! Sounds simple, right? But I had no idea how big this opportunity would become or the emotional roller coaster ride I would be on.

When the session ended, I thanked God for the opportunity, and got started.

Vince came to the next meeting to hear for himself what this excitement was all about. He agreed that I should go ahead. He thought it would fill my time while he was busy with his flourishing painting business. His business: the business that put food on our table and a roof over our heads, the business that I had grown to resent because it took so much time and energy out of my husband, who had become too tired to have fun with me.

In a way, he was right, though. With Vince away at work and our children out in the world making lives for themselves, it would be good to have something to do.

MLM will change your attitude and your life!

Are you ready for change?

I was happy to be busy meeting people and getting out of the house with a purpose. No more wasting time in malls, spending money on needless things that only provided temporary happiness! I invited my girlfriend Antoinette to come to the next MLM meeting. She decided to try the business, too. It seemed easy enough, after all. Like many of us in the MLM business, Antoinette didn't realize how difficult it would be to ask her family and friends for a favour.

I really took a liking to Natasha, the speaker at that evening's meeting. I became good friends with her, as we did not live too far from each other. I learned so much about the business world from her, and I felt comfortable asking her my many questions. Natasha could see my lack of belief in myself and encouraged me to believe I did have what it took to run my own business. She taught me how to market myself and my business. She gave me connections and suggestions as I learned about the business world.

The company offered a long distance phone service. My role was to ask family and friends to try it, and I eventually got paid. What a concept! And while at first I felt uncomfortable asking friends for a favour, I had to try, so I went to my Italian friends first. I was amazed when they said they would try my service! My service? What did I know about a telephone long distance service? Nothing! Yet they said they would help anyway!

I was amazed my Italian friends believed in me. I had no clue what I was talking about other than sharing my dream: to have another income in the wake of the fire, and for Vince to slow down so we could travel together.

Seeing that my Italian friends had been so accommodating, I started to feel I could handle being a multi-level marketer. So I started asking other friends and acquaintances. It was quite challenging when they said no or asked a lot of questions. I had a suggested script and got stuck when they asked something I did not have an answer to. Yet each time I made a sales call I got better and better.

My emotions were starting to sizzle. I began to feel alive again. Since things were going so well with our Italian friends, Vince decided to approach a few of his friends at work. One came to check out the business; he asked a lot of questions and created many scenarios using math. He went over and over and over it with

Vince, saying this could really be a big thing. It wasn't long before Vince's friend and his wife joined us for dinner, sharing that they both would like to own their own MLM business.

I soon got the courage to ask our accountants to be my customer. I made an appointment with them at their office. I was surprised when they walked into the boardroom with our business files. I just wanted to ask them to be my customer. As I was talking to them, I soon realized they were not interested in the service. I stood up, closed my brochure, thanked them for their time, and left the room. I was in shock. After faithfully using their services for eighteen years, all they had for me was a list of why they couldn't use my services! With my mind rehashing the incident as I was driving home, I ended up speeding. A police officer pulled me over. I was reduced to tears. As I waited for the ticket, I pulled myself together, gathering up enough courage to ask the officer, "Would you like to have some extra income?"

He replied with a firm, "No thanks!"

When I got home I told Vince that we were going to find a new accounting firm. "You can't do that!" he said.

"Watch me," was my retort.

Eventually we found a new accountant through the MLM business. The new accountant called our former accountant for our files. Surprised, they called me to ask why we would do such a thing after using their services for eighteen years. I explained I just didn't have the desire to continue supporting them — without their support in my business.

I decided I would ask my dentist to support my efforts. I made an appointment for five minutes of his time. He kept me waiting an hour, only to ask for a brochure. In following up, he informed me that he was not willing to change telephone carriers. I was not impressed at all, but I had put so much work into finding this naturally inclined dentist that I didn't want to start looking for another. I continued going to him, but I wasn't happy about it.

Proceeding with phone calls to my "warm" market (those whom I personally knew), I decided to try my church family. I sent everyone I knew personally a letter asking for their help. I was so naive in thinking my church friends would love to help me out. Reality check! You would think I had asked them to donate a vital organ. I was soon devastated when the majority said no, and gave me their opinions on the business. Rather than focus on the three people who agreed to become my customers, I chose to focus on the people who did not help me out. Instead of focusing on success, I chose to focus on rejection. My undisciplined mind was at it again.

I was incapable of handling so much rejection. I couldn't stay with that church after that and started on my search for a new church. When I found one, not even one member of my new church family became my customer. I had to worship somewhere, so I reluctantly continued. What did this all mean?

Sales professionals say our human nature is so negative; it often takes seven attempts to close a deal, to get people to say "yes." I began to know what that felt like!

By the fall of 2000, I was heavily into my new business, new church — and becoming a new woman. Beginning to feel the after effects of rejection and not feeling good about myself, I found myself calling Alesia, quite often in tears. She soon realized that I had an issue with self worth. It was just after my birthday that she sent me a poem along with her lovely email message.

Believe now, that you are a gift to this world and God put you here for a reason. You are a very special friend, and I would never want to leave this world without passing this on to you. Please treasure this note for a lifetime and never forget where it came from. I believe in you and am so proud, honoured and grateful that God shared His special gift with me.

Alesia's letter of encouragement was just what I needed. It kept me going when times were tough. I still treasure her note to this day. (See page 271 for the poem.)

After receiving her note, I realized some will, some won't, so what? Next!

I asked our lawyer and he said yes. Our drycleaner, florist, Italian grocer, a neighbour, coffee shop manager, financial investor, eye doctor, chiropractor, a few friends and a few family members said yes, too. God knew what I needed to learn from this, so all was well and within His plan for my life.

Chapter Three

Multi-Level Mission

When was the last time you did something
for the first time?

For years, I had felt empty, wandering in a sort of wilderness with no purpose, blaming someone else for my situation. That someone else always seemed to be Vince. It was his fault I had no life. It was his fault I was overweight, cooking and eating all that Italian food. It was his fault I was so quiet because he never shut up. It seemed that everything that was wrong in my life came back to Vince. But I loved him.

The one thing I hated most was being lonely. I knew I loved being around people because I had been running away from being home alone. I tried replacing my emptiness with shopping, but my outings and purchases left me unsatisfied. After one of my shopping trips, I would have more pretty clothes to wear, but nowhere to go and no one to go there with. When this MLM opportunity came into my life, I came to life, too.

I found attending the weekly business meetings and the Saturday training sessions very satisfying, whether Vince came with me or not. Vince said he didn't want to participate. He thought the business should be just for me, something for me to do. If it brought in a real income, that would be a bonus.

MLM turned out to be *a lot* of something to do. In addition to the weekly meetings and training sessions, I started going to seminars. I met Terri, a very interesting woman, at my first seminar. I liked her because she was a fully expressed person, not afraid to be herself or say exactly what was on her mind. She was a lot like Vince that way.

Terri and I eventually realized that we both had birthdays in April. We made a point of going out for dinner to celebrate. We found out that Natasha, another multi-level marketer, celebrated her birthday in April as well. A few more April ladies joined us in our fun. We shared lots of laughs together, we multi-level marketers of the Twenty First Century. We all wanted to change our lives and soar like eagles. We toasted ourselves and our goals at an Italian restaurant where Terri worked.

After attending all those meetings and seminars, I started to dream. My dreams were big dreams, dreams that had no limits, dreams that I was ready to make happen. I remembered how when I was a child I had wanted to be a dancer, on ice or in the ballroom, and a singer, and a movie star, and most especially I had wanted to be Miss Calgary. But I never had been those things. I had not believed in myself, had not believed I could have been any of those things, so how could I have started a plan to get there?

Well, now I had a goal, and an action plan. I wanted to be successful so that Vince could ease back on his working hours, and so that we could afford to retire in a few years. This was my ultimate goal, my driving principle. Then one day, I bumped into one of the builders Vince worked for. While in the mall, I told him about this phenomenal business I had got myself into so Vince could soon retire. But the builder looked at me kind of strangely, and told me, "Vince doesn't want to retire."

I had a hard time believing that, so a few days later I said to Vince, "You could retire in a couple of years if this business goes as well as they are saying. Then we could do some travelling and really have some fun!"

Vince replied, "I do not want to retire!"

Suddenly, my goal and plan for the MLM business had lost its foundation. I had thought I was building this business so Vince would not have to work so hard, and so that I could fill my time while waiting for him to have more time to spare. Now what? I would have to figure out for myself why I was doing this work. What was in it for me? The business would have to become my mission, not ours, and not his. In search of new motivation, I began reading.

I started reading a lot of books on MLM businesses, selling, the power of the mind, Internet businesses, how-to books – everything. I felt like a sponge. I was soaking up all the information I could.

As I read and learned more, and as Terri and I shared in conversation, our true feelings started to bubble up and rise to the surface. Terri told me about her challenge with cancer. I told her about my emotional struggles. Being true to our new friendship, I listened as she shared her reality. Terri heard my cries for help and encouraged me to see a counsellor to help me move forward. I agreed, knowing I had to get on with my life; I had to get on with my future. If I had to start opening up old wounds in order to heal, I was ready to do it.

When I approached Vince about going to a counsellor, he wasn't convinced.

"You don't need help, those people mess you up. For

sure, I'm not going," he announced.

I found myself disagreeing with him, something that rarely happened in the past.

"I *do* need help and I am going."

During my counselling sessions I opened up to hurt feelings buried deep inside and peered into dark corners previously denied. My reward was the discovery of a creative spirit that had long been ignored.

As I let go of some of my "stuff," my creative spirit slowly came to life. I found it very challenging stepping out of the familiar into the unfamiliar. I stayed with my counselling sessions until I became afraid to look back any farther. Then I stopped, ending them abruptly. My work was done, at least for now.

My short time in counselling, about four months, helped me set boundaries for my relationships at home. Vince still could not understand why I felt the need for a counsellor.

"Why can't you just be happy with who you are?"

I replied, "How can I be happy with who I am, when I don't know who I am?"

While reading and learning and looking inside, I'm sure I'll discover who I am, I thought.

Learning while working towards earning my own money was hard work. Vince worked very hard to provide for his family, far beyond the call of duty. He had grown up very poor in Naples, and wanted his own family in Canada to want for nothing. He wanted to provide everything for us. But to him, my working in MLM meant something was going dreadfully wrong with his plan, as apparently there was something he couldn't provide for me. "What's your problem? Why can't you just be happy with what you've got?"

I simply and truthfully answered, "I am happy with what I have, but there is a lot more out there I want to discover and experience."

Through MLM, I found a way in which to make things happen, and happen fast. MLM was a new way of doing business and earning money. I believed I was the chosen one, the pioneer designated to bring MLM to my family. I felt special and was reminded of my pioneer heritage. My Hungarian grandparents had risked everything when they decided to make the sea voyage across the ocean to Canada with their children. I began to see the importance of standing for something so I would not just fall for anything.

I came home excited after the weekly MLM meetings, so excited I wasn't able to sleep. My mind wandered all night, and I came up with many great plans. With just a few hours of sleep, I woke up in the mornings excited and ready to go. But go where and do what, you might wonder. I did not do anything extra. I just went about my normal business, doing things like going shopping, buying groceries, changing the oil of the car, picking up the dry cleaning, getting my hair done, and anything else that normally needed doing.

While I was out, though, anyone within three feet of me would hear about my MLM business, whether they wanted to or not! I had what multi-level marketers refer to as 'verbal diarrhea.' I hadn't learned about the MLM Valley of Death, where multi-level marketers go on and on and nobody else says anything, but I was fast approaching this new low. But I didn't notice, since I had something to be proud of. I had my first set of business cards.

I remember being with my family at a celebration years ago. A Hungarian realtor, a woman, came up to me and introduced herself as she offered me her business card. Oh, how I had wanted to have my own business card to show I was *somebody*, too! (See page 239 for my warning signals.) A few years before MLM, I had started a faux-finishing painting business and had made myself a set of business cards. I was *somebody* for just a brief time, as I didn't have those cards for long. Faux finishing was hard work, and I ended up coming home just as tired as Vince. This was definitely not the type of work I was looking for. Being tired every day was not part of my plan. I gave it up after a few months.

And now, thanks to MLM, I had my own business cards again. I was *somebody* again! With my phone number on my cards, I felt assured that people could now follow up with me about my MLM business opportunity. I didn't realize that most people did not call back.

I remember one incident at a local coffee shop. I bumped into a local hockey celebrity as he was fixing his coffee. Working up the nerve, I said, "Are you who I think you are?" He confirmed it and I was off, finally giving him my business card. I bumped into him three times, and each time I gave him my full presentation. He never called about this amazing business opportunity I had for him. Why he just stood there and let me ramble, I'll never know. And then there was the time we came back from Europe and we were standing beside the mayor's wife at the luggage corral. I just happened to have an envelope with information in it about the phenomenal business opportunity, and gave it to her while my heart was racing and my hand was shaking. Did she ever call me? No!

All I really wanted to do was have some fun. My family was busy. How could I have any fun staying at home by myself? I tried the "let's do coffee" thing but that did not satisfy my longing. Most of my friends were working, and anyone who was home wasn't available on the spur of the moment, which was how I often ran my life. I was used to being a workaholic mom, and left the house only when a moment of desperation compelled me to get out.

Then the day came when I got my first MLM cheque. I had my first "I earned this" paycheque in my own name, and it felt like I'd hardly done anything to get it, even though I had spent countless hours at meetings, training, seminars, and recruiting others to help me in my business.

I had not prepared a meal, had not cleaned toilets, had not ironed clothes, had not picked up after anyone, and I was getting paid. *I was getting paid.* I WAS GET-TING PAID!

I always kept my business cards with me. Three in each pants or jacket pocket, in my car, my hats, my socks and my purse. Some people might have said I was rather obsessive with my business cards. Vince would just roll his eyes when he saw me squirreling them away before we went out together. But it distressed him when the verbal diarrhea started; when I even stopped people I didn't know on the street to tell them the news about this MLM business. As if that wasn't enough, I left my business cards at phone booths, in books at the airport, in bathrooms, at ATMs, on car doors, on bulletin boards and at restaurants. Without exception, I mentioned the MLM business to everyone I met or came into contact with on the street, at a restaurant, in an elevator, or in a parking lot.

You get the picture?

Was it possible to run out of names of people to call about the MLM business? Hardly! We were taught how to expand our contact lists in an easy, systematic way. We were instructed to look through the yellow pages and, in alphabetical order by category, ask questions like, "Who do I know that is an accountant, a banker, a doctor, a lawyer, a repairman, a teller? Who do I know who has the same name as the accountant, banker, doctor that I know? Who do I know who knows an accountant, a banker, a doctor?" I was much more comfortable sharing with my cold market, people I did not know personally, than with my warm market, people I knew personally. After several cold and warm calls, after talking about my MLM business with everyone from complete strangers to dinner guests, I became an expert at scaring people off.

Despite the rejection I felt, the business had more positives to offer me than negatives. I had business cards, I was getting paid, and there was a lot of excitement in the air. I started talking to Vince about the big conference that was going to be held in Dallas, saying to him, "I would like to go to Dallas for the conference. Craig and Alesia said we could stay at their house, so it would cost us only the flight and registration fee. What do you think?"

Vince, in his usual unaccommodating manner when it came to MLM, said, "I'll think about it."

In my attempts to get Vince excited about the Dallas trip, I kept talking about it. Vince finally decided to ask his *paesano*, his home town friend Luigi, who was also

Antoinette's husband, if they would join us in Dallas. If Luigi and Antoinette were going to go, Vince would see the value in the conference, too. Luigi and Antoinette talked about it for some time and finally decided the Dallas conference would be on their agenda. Now the four of us would be on our way to Texas!

When we got to Dallas, we essentially went our separate ways. Vince and Luigi spent their time as tourists; teasing us about the "bull" we were learning. Despite our husbands' negative attitudes, we all managed to enjoy ourselves. Alesia and Craig were very good hosts, and dealt with our husbands' attitudes graciously. They made sure we saw as much of Dallas as possible, driving us around and showing us what old money and new money had created in the city. The best part of our trip by far was all the dining and entertaining at our new American friends' home.

While at the conference, Antoinette and I enjoyed all of the conference's professional development opportunities. In downtown Dallas, we watched in amazement at all the limousines dropping off the top money earners. We watched them coming and going throughout the hotel, striding with purpose, confidence and success.

There was a lot of excitement just being at the conference hotel. There was no lack of opportunity to spend your money either, what with all the promotional materials on dazzling display. Of course, I participated fully. You could even buy the entire conference program on tape, a great attraction since you couldn't possibly attend all the classes offered! I made sure I bought those as well, comforted in the knowledge that every expenditure was tax deductible.

In the mornings we would gather at the hotel for our training sessions, and in the afternoons we would go to a stadium for the motivational events. At these events we learned what the company was doing and watched lots of money being handed out to top earners who had met the requirements for incentive awards. Excitement rose as they walked across the stage to receive their bonus or acknowledgement of achievement. I found myself wondering how they achieved what they had achieved. It seemed like an impossible feat in my eyes. All the same, I left Dallas on a high, wanting to be able to achieve the same level of success. Money, fame and acknowledgement could all be mine, thanks to MLM!

Chapter Four

Multi-Level Me

Are you getting paid for what keeps you busy?

I thought I had been busy before, but now, recharged and motivated by the annual conference, I found myself busier than ever. I was excited after being in Dallas and too busy to think about what I was doing and whether it was getting me anywhere. My verbal diarrhea came out even faster and lasted longer. Now I had the shirts with the logos to stand out in the crowd.

I was used to being busy. Busy was my middle name! I was never bored at home when filling my days looking after children, entertaining, and volunteering. But whenever Vince and I went out, no matter where it was, somebody would recognize him. I was jealous of his popularity, which somehow reinforced my belief that I was nobody. In moments of despair, I dreamt of becoming a Proverbs 31 woman, a well-respected and highly prized woman of virtue and value, a hardworking woman with good business sense. I so longed to be known, recognized and loved—just like my lovable, huggable husband. I wanted recognition. I wanted to be valued. I worked hard at home and as a volunteer, but I never once earned the recognition in our community that my husband received. (See page 239 for my warning signals.)

No matter what I did, or how busy I was as a mother and homemaker, I had never been paid for any of the work I did. As a result, I wasn't familiar with connecting my works and making money. It seemed quite normal for MLM to keep me busy but not pay me a significant amount. I didn't notice anything wrong with this situation at all. Being busy with MLM continued, even though Vince was not so sure my participation in the business was worth my while or his.

I encouraged people to take a look at the business. A few did and were sceptical, and a few just kept me hanging. Those who hung there were the *maybes.* *Maybes* can kill you, figuratively speaking. As a multi-level marketer, you must have a yes or no answer, some kind of commitment. If you don't, you risk wasting a lot of time and energy. Between the no's and the maybes, I soon found out that people were not as excited as I was about the MLM opportunity.

Even some of my friends would not become my customers. A few came to see what the business was about, said it was not for them and wished me luck. When I asked a cousin, she, too, said no to being my customer. I did not know what to do after she turned me down. I stayed away from her until one day when she asked, "Dorothy, are you mad at me? I haven't heard from you in a long time."

"Actually, I am mad."

"What are you mad about?" she asked.

"I am mad that you won't be my customer."

We started to talk then, and between me sharing my feelings and her opening up to changing telephone carriers, I had a new customer and she had her cousin back.

I plugged along, being busy all the while. More and more, I found myself in the MLM Valley of Death. I gave too much information or just babbled on and on. Unsure of myself, I did not portray confidence in either my voice or body language when talking to others. This lack of assurance was certainly not conducive to sales. I was just excited and went on and on and on.

By now I had really taken an interest in the suggested books to read and started inviting more friends and family to the meetings to learn about this phenomenal MLM business. I even wanted to open up our home for meetings but Vince said, "No way! We are not having anyone come to our home. All these years you didn't want any of my clients to our home, so no way!" He was right. I had always felt that business life and family life should be separate.

Well, if they couldn't come to our home, then we would have to go to their home, I thought.

There was no way I was going to go into someone else's home by myself, so I convinced Vince to come with me. My first home visit was to show the MLM business to a young man in Banff, about an hour's drive away from Calgary. I had put an ad in that local paper and he was the first one to call. It was odd, having my husband sitting beside me quietly while I did most of the talking. We left our business prospect with no for an answer and chalked it up to experience, one we would never forget.

Vince was upset. "This is really stupid, driving all this way and sharing your real feelings and wanting to help people out and then they say no. I don't like doing this and I'm not going to do it again!" That was our first and last home visit with a stranger.

A few weeks later, a couple of door-to-door sales people arrived at our door. Of course, I asked them if they would like to hear about an awesome income opportunity. They said yes! I took their phone numbers and told Vince about the encounter. "I met these young people at our door and they would like to check out the MLM business. Do you think we could make an appointment and invite them inside?"

Vince was quite upset with me. "I thought we had an agreement: no people in our home!"

"Yes, I know dear, but we didn't like going to a stranger's home, and these people want to know about the business and they are in the neighbourhood. Just this once, okay?"

Vince relented. "Okay, just this once, as long as we are both here together."

Excellent, I thought. I made the appointment. When they arrived, I popped in the twenty-five minute video, thinking it would be straight and simple. No babbling on and on from my end, and afterwards they could ask me anything they liked. But the four of us sat there, ill at ease, as we watched the video. When it finished, they asked a few questions, and then they, too, said no. That was the end of strangers in our home.

As I built the business, a few business partners signed up and got to work, and a few signed up and did nothing. Even our missionary friends went to learn more about the MLM business in Houston. They thought it would be a great idea until they realized their shy dispositions would be a barrier to their success in the business. Desperate to generate some residual income, which is what MLM businesses are famous for, I was beginning to entertain thoughts of signing up family members into the business with me doing the work just to give myself a kick-start. Residual income in the MLM world is money that is paid to you month after month without you having to do any work. This residual income comes from business partners' customers, otherwise known as your down line.

I asked my son, Peter, to come and see the MLM business. A speaker was being flown in from the United States so he must be good, I thought. Tired of listening to me, Peter came. He said, "Okay, Mom, I'll come, but I'm not interested in this stupid business, okay?"

"Okay, Generation X son, but you'll learn about an easier way of making money. Just keep an open mind."

He brought his girlfriend with him, and they both

thought my fellow multi-level marketers were crazy. I suppose he was hoping that I would stop asking him about getting into the business if he came to one of the meetings. But I was relentless.

Peter and the rest of my family were getting tired of being embarrassed by me. At restaurants, I would mention the business to servers. At home, anyone who came over had to hear something about the business. It was impossible for others to escape hearing about MLM if I was in the room. My daughter, Melinda, was perhaps the most upset. We had just helped her buy a new car, and after the paperwork was signed, I started telling the salesman about the business and how he could create another income source. It was verbal diarrhea all over again. Both Melinda and Vince were quite upset with me over that incident. Melinda told me she couldn't have a normal conversation with me because of my obsession with MLM. "Mom, why are you letting this stupid business control you? I feel like I have lost my mom and I want her back!"

I tried to explain what was happening, at least as much as I understood it myself. "Melinda, I know it must seem strange, but I am having so much fun with the business, and I'm learning to communicate with Papa, too."

Melinda's anger continued, though. With Vince and I arguing, she felt stuck in the middle and resented me for causing all the problems. On Cloud Nine with the business, I was totally oblivious to what was going on around me, and completely unaware of the deep feelings of resentment that were arising in my children.

Unaware of these brewing storms on the home front, I continued to expand and promote the MLM business. I purchased a toll-free phone number to make it easier for people to find out about this extraordinary business, even while I was sleeping. People could call and listen to my very own three-minute message about the business. I had a lot of fun developing the message and changing it whenever I felt the need to do so. My excitement for the world of MLM was unwavering. I tried to coax family members to become business partners, saying I would pay for their start-up fees to get them going. But they weren't interested. Not taking no for an answer, I said that would be okay as I would do the work for them. My non-stop determination caused hard feelings between us and it did not work anyway.

Eventually, I realized that people who signed up also had to do the work. They had to have their own dream that would give them the passion to want to win at playing this MLM game of life.

We opened our home to my business partners, to thank them for their efforts. I congratulated them for getting started in their own business, which helped them as well as it helped me, hoping this might inspire them to give it all they had. That was what MLM was all about—helping yourself by helping others. I realized that not all people worked at the same speed. People generally had a hard time asking family and friends to be their customers. Putting trust into the company was an issue for many as well.

New recruits often did not realize there would be so many bumps along the way. The company's strategy was to have your family and friends become your loyal customers as their way of "helping you out" and, in turn, the company would benefit. I enjoyed what I was learning while being busy, busy, busy. Before I knew it a year had gone by. But, after a year of constant effort and expense, the money was nowhere near what I had thought I'd be making. Still, I continued pushing it.

Chapter Five

Multi-Level Moments

Is there something missing in your life?

I was so busy. The house was not getting cleaned. The dinners were simple, and sometimes they were getting burned. The fridge was not full. Vince was always saying something about how busy I was. Finally, I got tired of listening to him. Yes, I was busy. So was he! Why couldn't he see the similarity? Why couldn't he see that we were the same kind of busy people?

It was time to reward myself for being so busy. The business had taught me to think about myself and my wants. I decided to have a portrait taken. I found a photographer, brought along a statue that reminded me of freedom, and my statue and I had a photo session. This is cool, I thought. I sent one of the photos to the head office in Montreal to have it posted on my personal website. When I saw it there, online, I said to myself, "Look at that. I'm a real person with real feelings. I am somebody."

Yet something was still missing. Looking back, I realize that despite all the strides I was making, I was still afraid to be myself. On a subconscious level, I just wanted 2B Free 2B Me.

I remember that struggle. I knew that if I could just be me, I would be okay. I would be happy. I would not be depressed, or angry, or upset. If only I could just be me. (See page 243 for steps I took 2B me.)

I spent one night a week at the meeting where the multi-level marketers would bring their guests to see what the business was all about. I loved being a volunteer at the sign-in table, and shared my excitement with everyone who came. I listened attentively to the speaker each week, and slowly, I began to feel a new desire. I realized that I wanted to be at the front of the room, talking to people and sharing something valuable with them. I started dreaming of being a speaker. The dream became stronger as I started believing in myself, thinking I would have so much fun if I were up there, speaking. And it happened! Twice, I spoke when the leaders were out of town. On those happy days, I went to the front of the room for a few minutes to share what it was like to be a multi-level marketer in this company. And it felt so good! It didn't matter that the group was small. Really, there was nothing to be afraid of! I put on my apron, had my espresso cup in hand, and expressed how easy it was to sit down, relax, and enjoy your coffee while making long distance calls.

Here I was finally being able to 'espress' myself, being who I really knew I was and not who I thought I was.

My family was suffering from lack of attention. My pets were not receiving the same level of care as they had. The fish tank I had set up when our children were going through the terrible teens was dirty. My canary, Pavarotti, who had brought me much joy when he sang while we were home alone, was getting older, and I knew it would soon be time to say good bye. I told Vince that I wanted to give my pets away.

"You can't give your pets away; they give you so much pleasure."

"I know they do, but I want to spend more time building this new business."

Then it was summer. I said to Vince, "I'm not going to be doing any gardening this year, as I'm going to be focused on the business."

"What do you mean you're not doing the gardening? You love gardening! Are you sick in the head or what?"

"No dear, I'm not sick in the head. I just don't want

to be stressed out, so I am giving it up for a while."

Vince would not hear of the garden not being planted, so he decided he would do the gardening. He went out and bought the annuals, and bragged about how much he had saved compared to how much I had spent in the past. He started planting all the planters. I was so amazed. For twenty-three years I had done the gardening my-self, while Vince would complain about the cost of the flowers. And here he was, going out and buying them and planting them. What was going on here?

I began spending a lot of time on the Internet, learn-ing about my business and how to market it online. Sometimes, I lost track of time, and would come to bed very late, sometimes two or three in the morning. Vince was angry. A few times, he came quietly down to the office and startled me.

"What the heck are you doing in here, looking at porn?"

"I am **not** looking at porn! I'm learning how to oper-ate my business online! How could you think such a thing?"

I think that was when I lost my blindness, and be-gan to see clearly what I did not like about my husband.

We both became curious about the other's behaviour. The brick wall began to build between us. I began to get my back up, tired of his complaining. Being stressed out was no fun, and I was too busy with the business to do some of the things I used to do to the same degree of perfection. I asked him for some help with the house. Help, as in, a housekeeper. Vince's response did not surprise me. "We have two daughters!" I knew what that meant: arguments with them. That was not what I wanted. I told Vince that I was going to look for someone to help me around the house. He said, "Over my dead body you're looking for someone!"

In that time and place, I considered his words manipulation. He came from a poor and simple upbringing in Italy, and there was no way he wanted his money leaving our home to pay for a cleaning lady. But for me, enough was enough. I started looking for a housekeeper. In my mind, it was my money that would be spent, not his. I started on my new mission. I would pay someone to keep my house, and she would do what I asked her to do, just as Vince's employees did in his business.

When I'd found someone I wanted to meet, I brought the subject up again. "Vince, I found someone to help me clean the house."

Predictably, he exploded. "Over my dead body! Look at this will you? I have created a monster! Now you don't even listen to me! Look at you! I give you an inch and you take a mile! Did you hear me? Over my dead body you'll get a house cleaner!"

"Yes, I heard you. Are you hearing me?"

A few days later, we were at home with a repairman. There was a knock at the door. "Who's at the door?" Vince asked. He always asked that, as if either one of us could see through the walls. But this time, I knew who it was. The housekeeper, Lenička, was at the door. I let her in.

"Vince, this is Lenička, the housekeeper I told you about." Vince said nothing. He continued talking to the repairman, and I took her to see the house. As we went around, I told her, "I should warn you; my husband might raise his voice. He's not interested in having a house-keeper."

Lenička smiled. "My husband raises his voice as well when I do something he does not agree with." I was relieved. She understood.

After the repairman left, Vince did raise his voice, but neither Lenička nor I were surprised. Lenička and I finished our business, and she left, telling us how much her service would cost and when she could start. That was great for me, but not so great for Vince. He left the house immediately after, telling me, "You have no respect for me! This will be over my dead body!"

When he came home later that day with chest pains, and ended up in bed for two days, I was sure it had absolutely nothing to do with me not respecting him. I thought he had some deeper issue, but I had no idea what it was.

For me, it was all about standing up for something. This was the start of believing I was worth being heard. I realized that I had to take responsibility for asking for what I wanted, even in the face of fear. This was me re-teaching him how to treat me! God had helped me to look within myself, and helped me realize that it was my responsibility to acknowledge my needs. He had helped me realize that it was me, **only me**, who was stopping me from being myself. Because He helped me realize this, I knew that I would be able to stop being who everyone else wanted me to be. (See page 243 for steps I took 2B me.)

Soon, Vince came to see how Lenička enjoyed cleaning the house, and saw what a great job she did. He calmed down, let go of his anger, and saw how nice it was to have a clean home again.

As I learned how to use my voice, I became full of energy. I was beginning to be happy with myself. But Vince would still come home from work so tired and exhausted from running his business all day that he couldn't give me his full attention when I was sharing my excitement. The distance between us was becoming greater, and not much communication was going on. I remember thinking God had quite a sense of humour, having me in a communications business when I didn't know how to communicate with my own husband! I had grown up without good communication between parents and siblings, and then I ended up marrying the human equivalent of Mount Vesuvius. Vince always told me that he was never out of control like a real Neapolitan from Naples!

I kept going to the seminars and training, just to get away from the stress I was feeling at home, and to enjoy the upbeat people I was meeting. Then a miracle happened. Vince decided he would join me on the occasional training session, just to see what was going on in those meetings. He was hearing about it from me, as well as a friend from work. This friend had seen the big picture and had immediately got to work, and had created a good down line (people who start the business after you do).

I was ecstatic. The thought of the two of us being able to talk about MLM without becoming upset excited me. To help us rediscover our communication, I suggested we plan a vacation for just the two of us. Vince thought that was a great idea, so I planned a week's tour of Vancouver Island on the Internet for us, booking nights at bed and breakfasts, and going to other islands as well.

It was the first time we'd left our kids alone without adult supervision, but they didn't disappoint us. Vince and I had so much fun, just the two of us. I had all his attention, and he had mine! We fell in love again. It was great to see Vince relax and just be with me. We re-established our common language on that trip.

Chapter Six

Multi-Level Memories

Is your behaviour pushing away your loved ones?

Before I started my own business I had thought only about what I could do for others, but now I was thinking about what I could do for me. What was *I* worth? I had never thought about what I would like beyond being a stay-at-home mom and raising my children. That was what had kept me motivated all those years, giving to the family and providing a safe and happy place for them to grow up. Yet I had lost my identity somewhere along the way. Now I was thinking about goals. But what would I set a goal for?

When the time came for another training session I thought I could expand on what I wanted. I wanted Vince to come with me. I wanted to be able to share this with him.

"Vince, would you like to go with me to the Saturday training?"

"Training? Training for what? What do I need to learn? I need to learn nothing," he said.

Getting my back up, I replied, "Well, I want to learn

whatever they are teaching, so I will be going. It is this Saturday. I will be getting up early and I will not be home until five pm."

"Five pm! And what time does it start?" he asked.

"It starts at nine!" I yelled.

"What the heck have they got to teach about for eight hours?"

"I'll let you know when I get home!"

I sat comfortably at this training event, thinking about Vince at home, sleeping in, and telling me how stupid I was to be going to these things. The instructor asked us to consider how our relationships would look, if we were living life the way we wanted to. I remember thinking that there would be love, and lots of fun. But how could I get Vince to see things from that perspective? How could I get him to start thinking about living life the way both he and I wanted to? We had been beating each other up emotionally for so long. How was I going to get him, my Romeo, to consider learning something about relationships when he wouldn't even go to a session about owning your own business?

But maybe he was right. What did he *need* to learn about having his own business? He had started his own in 1979, without any training whatsoever. He just got tired of working for someone else. He was an entrepreneur. So maybe he didn't need any training, but I sure did! I wanted to learn, and learn everything I could. I was not going to be sleeping in on any Saturday. I was going to keep myself very busy with this business.

I did keep myself very busy. I kept my mind busy, too, thinking about things I had never done before, and discovering what things I actually liked. I bought myself a ring with my birthstone in it. I had never bought anything so nice for myself, and even though it was pricey, I felt that I was worth it! I also bought a vanity licence plate for my car, and all with the money I was earning. When the time came for my birthday, I decided to go for a hot air balloon ride. I invited Vince, a brother, and our accountant. It was amazing to be up so high, looking over the city I had lived in my whole life. I was soaring to new heights as a Calgarian, and enjoying the new me, too.

Out of the blue, Vince surprised me for my birthday. He gave me 47 roses. He had never bought me flowers before. He said they were a waste of money, and they die. Yet he gave me roses. And I could not have cared less. I used to love flowers. Now, I thought they were a waste of money too.

But the gift opened my eyes to some of the ways that Vince was changing. Before, it had been his opinion, and his opinion only, that carried weight. Now, he actually seemed to have some consideration for my opinion.

He wasn't changing in every way, though. He continued ridiculing me about the business, especially when I went to the registries office to incorporate it. When I started the business, I had included his name on the application as one of the proprietors, and now included his name when I incorporated the business as well. Why did I do that? I wondered. What was I afraid of? Why did I feel it was necessary to include him? I got angry, and told him he did not deserve to have his name on the business. I asked him to remove his name as a director of the company I had created. I would be a millionaire by myself! He laughed. Inside, I was struggling. In the end, I just stomped off.

I decided to sign up for a financial seminar so I could learn what to do with all that money that would be coming in. The cost of the tuition included your spouse, so I invited Vince to come along, and he did. There, we bumped into a carpenter friend of his who was at the class as well. His friend was listening to all the big plans I had, then looked at Vince and said, "She has got too much time on her hands!" To which Vince agreed! I felt sorry for both of them. They were stuck in the rat race and had no time at all to either plan their lives or enjoy them.

At this seminar, I was given two tickets to another seminar. Having just finished one, Vince was not interested in going to something else, but reluctantly joined me once again. This one was on a much bigger scale and dealt with how limited our minds are. I found it very interesting, and signed up for the weekend seminar. It was something new, and I soaked it all up.

Still excited about growing my business, I went my way and Vince went his. Within a short time, Vince was expanding his business as well. Our friends, Urs and Iris, who were both painters, came to him with an offer he could not refuse: build a duplex with them. I wished them all luck, and made sure they knew that I would not be involved. I would be spending all my efforts on my own business.

They were quite shocked, both because I was not

willing to help out in any way, and also because there was no room for negotiation. Even though I would not participate, the three of them agreed to be partners, and bought an old house in the district of Banff Trail. They knocked it down to build the duplex.

Throughout this building project, I continually heard about Urs and Iris, the Painter Couple, doing the project together while he was on his own. I countered with names of MLM couples doing business together while I was on my own. This did not please Vince at all, and we really started arguing. And while arguing didn't make me happy, I couldn't turn back into the person I had been. I didn't really like who I was now, but going back would be even worse.

As I continued to build my business by attending the never-ending training sessions, excitement started to build around the upcoming annual conference in Dallas. I said to Vince, "I am planning to go to the annual conference. Would you like to join me?"

"Are you kidding? I went last year. No way are you going to get me to go over there and waste my time again," he said.

So I left it at that and continued on my learning

curve. I was now learning how to be involved in conference calls and started buying leads for my business. Leads were names and phone numbers of people who had responded to an advertised questionnaire in magazines regarding interest in home based businesses. I was extremcly excited about calling people I did not know, but was shocked that not many were positive leads. But there were still a few people who showed interest, and I invited these people to a conference call on the Internet, where a speaker would explain about the business. I liked this process because I thought it would make it easier to close the deal, but not so. I learned after many months that it was a numbers game, just like calling people I knew. The morc people you called who said NO, the closer you got to a YES. But I was getting tired. How long would I be willing to play the game?

Coffee Break Thought

What would my
life look like
if I was the
Master of my
Mind?

Chapter Seven

Multi-Level Mess

Do you know your heart's desire?

Vince came up with an idea, "How about we go on a European tour and go see my family for the festa dei Gigli?"

"Would that be before or after the annual conference?" I asked.

"Are you still thinking about that stupid thing?"

"Oh yes I am, dear," I said.

"Let's forget about that and just go to Europe as a family. We can't afford to do both," he said.

I considered it, but all I could remember was our last family holiday from hell. "I thought we were not going on any more family vacations because of the disaster with the last one."

"Well, things have changed," he said. "The kids are older now, and can do whatever they want. And so can we! It would be so much fun!"

But I wanted to go to the annual conference in Dallas. We had been to Europe many times visiting family over the years. Every time we went, I had asked if we could rent a car so we could get around easier. The answer was always the same: we could not afford to rent a car. And yet this time, he was renting a car in Germany and touring until they got down to Naples where his family was. Here I was being offered my heart's desire — and I refused!

I gave up the European trip to go to the annual conference in Dallas. Vince would take the kids on a European tour. While they were gone, I would try to figure out if it was easier living with the loneliness of them away, or of them being home and busy with their lives. I would have two and half weeks of doing whatever I felt like until the conference.

My children each tried to convince me to join them, but I said they could enjoy themselves without me. So I wished them a fond farewell, and dropped them all off at the airport, giving them a hug and kiss goodbye.

I remember struggling with my feelings over that decision as I was driving home alone. I behaved like I was in a coma; I was there but I wasn't. I came back home, wondering why I had chosen to put them on a plane without me. Yet I realized it would be a good experience for me. I had poured my whole life into my family. I had no idea what life was like on my own, so it was time to try hanging out with me. Me, myself, and I, we would get to know one another.

Silence took on a different quality when I knew that no one would be coming in the door for three weeks. Our home had been quiet for many years now, at least during the day. But during this time, I was in charge of how I spent my day. I did not have to report to anyone. I did not have to feel guilty if the house was untidy, or if dinner was not prepared and I ordered in Chinese food. I just chose to enjoy myself.

So I enjoyed the quiet house. I enjoyed listening to my relaxing music while having a bubble bath for as long as I wanted. I enjoyed talking on the phone as long as I had things to say. I enjoyed visiting people who Vince never felt like visiting, and stayed as long as I wanted to. I enjoyed reading and watching movies. I enjoyed going for walks along the river at whatever time of the day I felt like. I enjoyed my freedom of choice. But then I realized that I always *had* freedom of choice! They were always my twenty-four hours, with or without my family. What an eye opener that was! *I* was the cause of my own guilt!

Yet while on those walks, I saw couples and young mothers with babies, and here I was all alone, with memories of the happy days past when I had enjoyed being a stay at home mom with stay at home children. Now the stay at home children all wanted to stay in their own homes, and start their own lives. I was happy for them, but felt lost in the shuffle. I felt too old to be a young woman, but too young to be an old woman! When would I become a grandmother, and would that moment allow me to once again be comfortable with my life? Or would it? When would I fall in love with myself, know I was significant, and look at myself as God saw me?

After enjoying all that time alone, I had five days to enjoy myself in Dallas. Even though I stayed at the hotel this time, Alesia took me out for lunch just about every day. I enjoyed the classes and meeting new people, but I was torn. I felt as though I did not belong there and I did not like being alone either.

When the conference was over, I became part of Alesia and Craig's hectic life for two days. My eyes were opened to this different type of family: double income, no kids, two dogs, and a swimming pool in the back yard. They were professionals. While they had given up the MLM business, we were still friends. It was a real treat to stay with them and see their lives in action.

Vince called me a few times while he was away. He seemed to be having a great time with the kids and visiting with his family, but for some reason, our conversation was always cool. I had realized that I was angry at how my life had turned out, and angry that I had not gone to work part time many years ago, so that I could feel like I belonged in the world. My thoughts of not fitting in went even further: I was too Italian to fit in with my Canadian friends, and too Canadian to fit in with my Italian friends! It seemed like I didn't belong anywhere. It also seemed I was blaming Vince for my life or lack of life, because he said he did not want me to go to work, even after the kids started school. I had been very happy being a stay at home mom until the last one went off to school. But that was around the time I started to get depressed. I had been so busy taking care of the family and now there was no one home. I had wanted more out of life but I didn't know what, or how to get it!

Vince had bought a ring for me in Europe. It was to have commemorated our twenty-fifth year of marriage, which we would be celebrating in November 2001. I picked up the family from the airport on September 7, and we drove home. Something wasn't right, though. When we got home, he threw the ring at me, saying, "I hope you are happy now!" What was he talking about? I *wasn't* happy! But I didn't know how to fix it so that I *was*!

I had invited some friends over for dinner the day after Vince's return, but he woke up still quite upset and tired from the long trip. He was not interested in visiting with anyone. He left the house while I was getting ready for our company. What could I do? I had never let on to anyone about our arguing. How was I going to pull this off without mentioning it?

I tried. With a smile, I told each of them, "Vince will not be joining us for dinner tonight. No, no, nothing's wrong." But that line didn't cover it. All the guests were Italian, and when it came time to eat, they all said they would not eat without him.

Dinner was ready, but there was no husband, and six people were calling him on his cell phone, trying to talk him into returning home to talk things over. These couples were all older than we were, so I hoped that he would listen to some of their advice. But he was stubborn. He assured them he wasn't coming home, and they should go ahead and eat without him. They still refused. They kept calling him on his cell phone until he agreed to come home. By the time we sat down to eat, several hours had passed. It was a day none of us would ever forget.

Whatever was going on in our marriage had reached the exploding point. Two days later, we decided to get a divorce, our twenty-fifth anniversary present to ourselves. We put the house up for sale on September 10, 2001.

The next day, two planes flew into the World Trade Centre in New York.

Chapter Eight

Multi-Level Madness

Mirror, mirror on the wall,
why did my life turn out this way?

A few weeks had gone by. There was a lot of tension in the air. The house had not sold. We received word that there was a death in the family. We decided we would patch things up. I went to see a counsellor. After listening to me for a while, he told me, "Dorothy, it would be good for you to learn to express yourself in a *positive* way."

Now, *that* was a good idea. How come I had never thought of it?

I started to look forward to learning how to communicate in a positive way. After a few visits, I got the courage to ask my family to join me. They did not want to come, but I asked them to do it for me. The counsellor asked them each a few questions, they answered them, and that was that. They didn't need to come with me again. I was there because I wanted to be there, so I continued alone, but I was happy that they had come to support me, even briefly.

One thing became clear in counselling. I had had

twenty-five years of practice in our marriage and an additional lifetime of practice blaming other people for events in my life. I blamed my parents, my boss, my friends, my husband, my children—everyone. It was always someone else's fault. But finally, the counsellor got me on the right track. I started looking within, and also focusing on biblical principles and promises. I knew this would help me, and I was ready to excel in my marriage as well as my business. I knew that the only one I could change was me. I couldn't change my family.

Then I got too deep. I came close to something about myself that I was afraid of. When that happened, I panicked. I cancelled my next appointment, and then another, and then I just stopped calling. Inside I knew I was afraid of something, but I didn't know what it was.

Throughout my counselling sessions, Vince complained about the cost. He made sure to voice his opinion about not having my kind of spare time, as he was finishing up his duplex project and was getting ready to start his second one. This one he would be doing with our daughters; I was not invited to participate because I had insisted on building my MLM business. Vince and the girls were on their own, and so was I.

With my family busy, I continued on my quest for further learning. Speaking was next on the agenda. Since the counsellor had taught me more about communicating clearly on a personal level, I thought that I might as well learn how to speak professionally as well. I invited a friend to go with me to a leadership seminar on speaking. She was nervous about speaking in public as well, wanting to learn a few tips to help her out at church. We shared a few laughs as we learned what to do and what not to do as a speaker, and how to speak about something spontaneously. We were well prepared after the seminar, prepared to notice all the mistakes another speaker would make!

My extremely aggressive behaviour had pushed my family farther and farther away from me. It was good for me to learn how to communicate in a new way. On my personal growth journey in MLM, I became aware that I was *reacting* to everything and everyone. Not only in my business, in my everyday life as well. I stayed away from anyone who did not want to listen to me. Not being able to find people who were interested in doing this business, I felt the need to keep myself busy anyway. The business was doing well and really growing without any of my help, but I just couldn't relax. Vince was so busy with his job and now the duplex project. I had said I wanted to expand the business. How could I just sit back and relax now? I started looking for new customers. I asked a few more of my cousins to become customers. One said no. One said she was on the service already. But one said yes! It felt good to have someone say yes and she was the one I thought for sure would say no!

When she did, she asked me, "How long have you been doing this business?"

Truthfully, I told her, "I have been doing this for a few years."

"Why did it take you so long to ask me?"

"I... had to learn how to handle my emotions, first, because I found that there was a lot of rejection in this business."

I was hesitant to start making phone calls again, simply because I did not want to risk hearing *no*. But I had to learn how to handle rejection. If I didn't, I was going to lose the people I loved. I had already left my church once. I was not going to leave my family.

To cope with rejection, I began to compare myself to a waitress. When a waitress asks you if you want coffee, and you say no, you are rejecting the coffee, not the waitress. What I found, though, is that when it happens over and over again, you forget about the coffee. The feelings and emotions come into play and all kinds of weird dialog starts happening in your head. Pretty soon you don't even realize what's going on, but you know you feel bad about yourself. You just have to keep telling yourself that when people say no to your request; it's about them, not you. We say no seven times before we are able to say yes. Why is that? Even for myself, *no* is my automatic response!

Then I reached a turning point. I asked Leslie, a cherished friend of mine, to be my customer. And she said no. For a moment, I was torn. The choice was between making and breaking this important relationship because she had said no. But I didn't have to think long. I decided right then and there that I would no longer allow the MLM business to destroy any of my friendships! I would take full responsibility for my feelings. I chose to understand her reasoning, and let go and loved her anyway.

I challenged myself by attending seminars out of town that were not in the MLM industry. I wanted to learn about fears and how to overcome them. I was beginning to realize that my fears were holding me back from real living. Vince was very uncomfortable with me going to these seminars. He called them brain washing. I heard him voice his opinion, but I went anyway. I was on a mission. What kind of mission I wasn't sure, but I was definitely on a mission!

Following one of these seminars, I felt it was time for Vince to challenge himself, too. I bought him a set of CDs by a famous speaker. He didn't like reading, but he could listen to the CDs while doing his exercises. It took a few months before he would even open the package, but when he did start listening to them, he felt inspired to do something he hadn't done before.

"Let's go to San Francisco for the weekend," he said. "I have always wanted to go to San Francisco."

"I had no idea you have always wanted to go there!" I replied. Mamma Mia! I could hardly believe it! If that was all it took to get Vince to think about doing something he hadn't done before, imagine the results if he had come and been open minded at any of the seminars!

But while I continued going to the seminars, Vince

continued with his cynical attitude. My emotions were on a roller coaster ride due to rejection in the business, and he didn't like seeing it. He decided that MLM was stupid. MLM was a topic that brought a lot of anger into our home, so we just left it alone. But that wasn't good enough either. I had come from a broken family, and I had said I would never put my children through that pain. But here we were a family in pain anyway. Staying together was painful, and so was separating. Which would be better?

"Vince, I'm tired of this entire BS game we play with each other. I think it's time we split up for good. I would like to move out."

"That's not possible. We made a commitment, and we're going to stick to it. Besides, the kids need you."

"The kids need me? How can you say that! They're hardly here! They don't need me at all, and you don't need me either. Besides, we see things so differently now. We are never on the same page anyway. Why do you want to keep going with this ridiculous life?"

I said we could get together on weekends, and he started teasing that he would build me a house. Although I did not laugh at his suggestion, I did say to him that I did not need him or his money. Ours had become a marriage of cynicism, and I was beginning to feel it would be for the best for our family if we did separate.

We told our children that we could not take it any longer, and that we were driving each other crazy. We told them that our marriage of love/hate had to come to a stop for the sake of our sanity. I was hoping they would accept it because of being tired of all the fighting that had gone on over the years, but not so. Josephine was overseas, but we sat down with Peter and Melinda.

Peter was very sad when we told him. He didn't say much to me. But I did hear him say to Melinda, "Where can Mom go? She doesn't have any money."

Melinda was angry. "I wish this MLM business had never come into our lives!" Then she asked a very important question. "Mom, how much money are you making with this MLM business anyway?"

I responded with the truth, "One hundred and fifty dollars a month residual income."

She was shocked. "Mom, how can a marriage come to an end because of a hundred and fifty dollars a month?" she asked.

"It's not about the money, Melinda. It's about Papa

not liking who I have become," I said.

Life was tough. We continued tolerating each other while we tried to decide what would be best. I did my thing, and he did his, and we stayed married with children. We did not want our children to have to live with the shame of a broken family. We loved each other, but hated each other, too. How long could our marriage last?

Vince focused on his business and I focused on mine. Life went on. I felt that we really needed to work on our marriage, not on our businesses, but when one will and one won't, what can you do? So I just kept busy.

Even though there was turmoil in our marriage and we kept busy with our businesses, we still did something for our anniversary. We planned a trip to Las Vegas with our friends Antoinette and Luigi. We had a great time walking and talking and dancing in front of the Bellagio hotel. There was a water show on the strip with Celine Dion and Andrea Bocelli singing.

Wow, how lucky we were to be in Las Vegas, having fun with our friends. We said thank you to God that we'd made it through another year.

Chapter Nine

Multi-Level Money

Are your actions so loud that
no one can hear a word you're saying?

We seemed to have a lot of fun when we went away, and we forgot that we weren't getting along at home. So we decided to go visit our favourite place in Canada: Victoria. It was January, and cold, even though Victoria is usually the warmest place in Canada. But to us, it didn't matter. We still enjoyed the sights, sounds, and smells, and going for walks along the ocean.

In addition to MLM, I was also the secretary for Vince's painting business. Shortly after arriving home from Victoria, I decided to get started on our T4 slips for tax season. I celebrated when it was done. It wasn't one of my favourite things to do.

Then Vince came home, tired from a hard day's work. He looked in shock at the dollar amount on our T4 slips. "How could this have happened?" he yelled. "Where did all that money go? How could we have spent that much money?" He continued to yell at me, and when he was finished, I went to my bedroom and cried.

When I woke up in the morning, still unhappy about what had happened, I said to myself, "That's it. Enough is enough." I wrote Vince a letter of resignation.

When he came down in the morning, I said to him. "Vince, if I worked for you in the real world, you would be charged with harassment for the way you treated me last night."

"Oh, get real," he said. "Now let's sit down and see where all the money went."

"No," I said. "I'm not interested in sitting down with you and talking about the T4s. Here is my letter of resignation." I handed him the letter. "I quit."

He hit the roof. So did I. We continued in a heated discussion of put downs, yelling and screaming. But in the end, I had quit, and now only had one job: my own business.

The business was growing without my help, and that meant that the residual income was increasing. There was enough to continue paying Lenička to clean the house. I could do whatever I wanted, so I decided to become an employee. I felt that if I worked outside the home, I could meet more people, and have the chance to tell them about the MLM business. It would also give me something constructive to do, something where there would be no rejection!

I started working on a resume and looking in the paper for a job. I could not believe I was doing such a thing. I knew what it was like to work for someone else, but here I was, looking to do exactly that!

I interviewed for a temp agency, but I didn't have enough knowledge of the latest computer programs used in offices. The temp agency didn't know me, and didn't care that I got honours in typing. I was a little frustrated by that. Just because I didn't know the programs didn't mean I couldn't learn them!

In the end, I found a job cooking at a senior's residence. Of all the jobs I interviewed for, I knew I would be best at that one. Seeing as I was not cooking much at home anymore, I found this new job exciting. I was around people. They appreciated what I did for them. It was fun, for a while. When I first started working, one of my friends had said I would last three months. How had she known? It was just after three months that I started complaining about the job. I felt I did not have enough time for my business. How would I fix this?

I decided to have my very own website so the business could build itself, and I thought it would make a nice birthday present from me to me. I asked one of my cousins to help. She was a website designer, so I thought between her and I, we could come up with something good. She listened attentively as I explained what I wanted, and I told her to do her thing. She did, but she always came back asking me to figure out *exactly* what I wanted. I had trouble understanding. I knew we were both speaking English, but I did not understand her lingo and she did not understand mine. It was frustrating on both ends, but eventually we learned to speak each other's language and the project came together: www.BeyondExplanation.com.

I was having fun because I was doing exactly what I wanted to do. But if I was having fun, why wasn't I happy? Some of my MLM acquaintances had won trips to Mexico through the company's incentive program. I hadn't quite qualified for the trip, however, and was starting to feel sorry for myself. I wanted to go to Mexico!

"Vince, I am working so hard, and it's just not quite working. Whenever we go away and enjoy some time, just you and me, it is because I plan it. When are you ever going to take the initiative?" I asked.

A few days later, he showed me a trip plan for Mexico. I was surprised. "How am I supposed to go to Mexico, when I've only been working for a few months?"

"Just quit your job. You don't need that job anyway," he said.

I got excited about going to Mexico. I told my boss that I needed a week off, as my husband had planned a surprise trip for us. To my surprise, she had no problem with that. We left for Mexico and had a great time. While I was there I tried parasailing. I was afraid, so I didn't look down. I just looked across and saw things in the distance from up high. While up there, I sang one of my favourite children's hymns to enjoy the ride.

We loved meeting friendly people from other cities. A couple from Toronto bought me a little gift for my birthday and joined us for dinner to celebrate. It felt like a new stage in our lives, doing something on our own. When I came back, I told my boss I would be quitting in two weeks. I had lasted four months at the job.

But it wasn't a new stage; it was only a vacation. I was becoming an expert at complaining. Vince was getting good at it himself, complaining that it was my fault that he was stuck figuring out all the paperwork for the business. Vince complained about me, and I complained about him. Complaining, blaming, justifying, and defending seemed to be the norm around our home. I was getting tired of playing this marriage game and wanted to spend less and less time with my husband, so I left him complaining and moved on with my life and my business.

I started going to different networking luncheons, speaking about my business and meeting people for coffee to show them the business. I had found from the training sessions that people were having more success with prospective business partners after having a one-on-one presentation as compared to bringing them into a group meeting. A one-on-one meant that I would meet with one person and explain the business. If the prospective business partner was interested, I would invite him or her to a much larger group meeting.

I bought myself a laptop and learned how to do a PowerPoint presentation. I was on a roll, enjoying learning, once again expanding on my business. But I found that people didn't always show up when they had an appointment. I would call as I was waiting for them, and there would be no answer. I would call back the next day, and still no answer. I wondered why people could not just say no if they were truly not interested. What were they afraid of?

Some time later, Alesia and Craig called us up and asked us to go on a cruise with them, to help them celebrate Alesia's birthday. What an offer! Getting away and doing something new might bring some spark back into our marriage, I thought. Vince seemed to agree. We both got excited, as we had never been on a cruise before. Vince kept busy at work and I started planning for the trip. I enjoyed shopping for the right clothes to wear. I had a lot of fun buying gifts for Alesia, too. I would give her a birthday gift at breakfast, lunch, and dinner. I felt so alive and had so much fun on the trip. I was up and at it early in the morning, going for breakfast with my American friends while Vince slept in and relaxed before joining us upstairs. It was great to see him relax and enjoy himself. With our sponsors no longer in the business we did not talk business at all. We all just relaxed and had fun enjoying the Western Caribbean.

We came home, and as I continued working on the business, I began dreaming, reading, and making new goals. I had a long list of goals. Buy a downtown building to open a coffee shop in memory of my mom. Go on a holiday whenever I wanted to. Travel around the world. Buy my sister a new car, buy my brother a new truck, and buy my dad a new car, too. Take my in-laws to Hawaii. Buy an airplane. Hire a limo driver. Have the most beautiful weddings for our daughters. Buy extravagant gifts for my customers. Pay someone to come in and set up an office just for me with top-of-the-line technology. Buy nice clothes. Buy a hot tub and pay someone to take care of it. Buy an elaborate fish tank and pay someone to take care of it. Buy a few birds and pay someone to take care of them, too. Hire a gardener to take care of the yard. I found it an amazing experience to expand my mind while expanding my business.

Chapter Ten

Multi-Level Music

Do you know what you have to do for you?

Besides his career in painting, Vince had a passion for soccer. He was the assistant coach of a team that would be competing in a tournament in Spain in a few months. Vince planned on going to the tournament, and then visiting family in Italy. With those plans in the works, I decided to do something that I had wanted to do for a long time. I found an Italian teacher to teach me Italian. I thought it would also be a good idea, since I was going to Spain as well, to learn Spanish, too. Little did I know! By the time I got to Europe, I could not speak at all. All I knew was that I was not supposed to speak English. I was so confused with the other two languages that I froze. But I only froze when I had to speak to an Italian or Spanish person. I remember having a blast on that trip, spending ten days with family in Italy and ten days in Spain. I celebrated my birthday in Spain over a platter of fresh seafood and sangria. I wore my Canadian jacket, and my T-shirt with my website address embroidered on it. The MLM Company had expanded into Europe creating even more excitement. It was a great time to share with Europeans what was opening up in their country. Just like Alesia had done with me back in December 1999. I took every opportunity to talk about my business while on that trip, handing out my Canadian flag pins.

It was spring in Europe, a bit chilly and windy. A few foreigners and the local young people braved the beach on the weekends. We had time after the tournament to tour for two days. As I was letting go of the old me, I started noticing things more. I was waking up from my emotional coma. I felt as though I had a new pair of glasses on. I had a greater appreciation for what was going on around me. I saw beautiful people interacting. We took a boat taxi from town to town, and I noticed a few topless sunbathers who hung around just where these taxi boats would land. I thought those women were sure free to express themselves!

With three and a half years gone by, the residual income finally started kicking in. Every month it increased. Vince seemed to think this money was coming from heaven. He sure did not understand how residual income worked, but he liked it.

MLM had taught me to imagine how my life would be if all the bills were paid and I had all the time I wanted. Well, all the bills were paid by my husband's income. I had twenty-four hours in which to do what I wanted. So I chose to spend, spend, and spend more.

I signed myself up for a seminar in Vancouver. I wanted to learn how to be a speaker. The participants were asked to prepare something to do on stage—something outside of their comfort zone. How could I do something like that? Surely I was going to be judged! But I had signed up, so I did it anyway. I decided to dress like a hippie and sing a song on stage. I started doing some research on the Internet and came up with a costume idea. Then I approached a seamstress who lived in the neighbourhood. She gave me some further suggestions. I bought the supplies, she started sewing, and I started singing. I remember having so much fun working on the project, choosing the song I was to sing, and getting the costume ready. It was so much fun dancing with no one watching. I had always wondered what it would have been like to be a hippie when I was a teenager in the Sixties. Now I had my chance to be a hippie for an evening!

A month before it was time for me to fly out, Vince decided he would drive out after me, along with our friends Luigi and Antoinette. We could all visit their paesano in Vancouver and drive back together. That sounded like fun. I made sure he knew, though, that I would give him my full attention once the seminar was completed, and not before.

The seminar was amazing. We were coached on how to overcome our fears of speaking and performing. We were taught to define what our own comfort levels were. Just before the stage event each evening, we were warned to leave the room if we were offended by any-thing, but the performances would go on. I was having too much fun hanging around people who really wanted to move forward in their lives. I ignored what I didn't like and stayed for the evening.

And then it was my time. I remember being so afraid, I thought I would faint as I stood next in line. I listened to the coaching being whispered in my ear, took a deep breath, and I went on. I looked at everyone. And then I danced and sang as though no one was watching me, just like I did when I was practising at home. It was so powerful. It opened up a part of me I had never known. I was so encouraged by my willingness to overcome a fear that I had had for such a long time, and it was humbling in the end to stand there accepting the applause.

Vince, Luigi, and Antoinette had driven ten hours through the Rocky Mountains, and arrived with an evening and a day to look around while I finished up at the seminar. We had dinner together on my break, and Vince seemed quite nervous. Unknown to me at the time, he had talked to another participant of the seminar in the parking lot. This fellow told him about the performances, and how every individual's level of comfort was different. Vince, the protector of the family, did not like the idea of that. It was as though he was the father of a teenager, not the husband of a grown woman!

After the last performance finished and the seminar was coming to a close, Vince walked into the room looking for me. I was walking around hugging those I had come to know, exchanging phone numbers. I introduced Vince when he found me, and he seemed to keep a close eye on all those hugging people. I was on a high. Vince was on a low.

We headed off to our room to get ready to visit our Vancouver friends. He started asking me a lot of questions. I told him I was tired, and asked if it could wait until after we had gone visiting. I was emotionally exhausted from the weekend, but what I had learned at that seminar was put to good use, even that very weekend. I learned that, as a speaker, *you* are in control of the room, and you do not have to answer any questions if you choose not to.

When we came back from our friend's house, he started asking me questions again. I told him I was exhausted, and would answer his questions in the morning. I remember feeling like I was being interrogated. I had done nothing wrong, and told him so. I had been afraid of him since we married, and had never stood up to him like that before. I really had to go out of my comfort zone. He did not like my answer, and it showed loud and clear.

By morning, he was dealing with his emotions. I still didn't know what was going on, and neither did our friends, who had the privilege of a ten-hour drive back to Calgary with us. I really didn't feel like having any conversation, so I kept pretty quiet. When we reached Lake Louise, we stopped to look at the beautiful scenery. I chose not to walk and hold hands with him. He was back to normal, but I was just beginning to go over in my mind what had happened back there in Vancouver. When we arrived home, it took a week of talking about what had happened, so that we could be friends again.

We both let go, forgiving each other once again. Vince and I did not talk much about the seminar after that. For a while, anyway, until I mentioned that I would like to attend another seminar with that same organization. He had one answer. "Those people are absolutely nuts, and my wife will absolutely not be going there again," he said.

I chose to back off, forever carrying the memory of being on stage. Peace was more important than insisting on having my way!

Chapter Eleven

Multi-Level Message

Are you ready to wake up and smell the coffee?

Summer was the hardest time of the year for me to cope with life. Vince was the busiest, and the kids were working full time. I decided that I was not going to work at my business full time that summer. I went to the meetings only occasionally. I was no longer at the sign-in table or volunteering in any way. I was discouraged with everything. This business was hard work. I was struggling with my emotions.

I was tired of talking to people. I was confused from listening to my undisciplined mind. I was complaining about my life. I was spinning in circles. The money was coming in, but my family could not have cared less. I was no longer passionate about MLM. I needed to start asking myself some serious questions about what I wanted to do with my life.

I knew I liked to have fun and travel. I started talking about going to Dallas once again for the annual conference, thinking that might re-ignite my excitement. We had fun there the first time. Second time I went alone. We missed the next year because of going on the cruise with Alesia and Craig. Now, Vince and I would both be going to the annual conference together. Were we going as a team? I sure hoped so. I remember thinking that all this personal growth was having an influence on my loveable huggable husband; I had had no troubles convincing him to go.

I suppose he was coming to protect me from the real world. Or was he coming to get an understanding of how this money kept coming and coming? The residual income was catching his attention. Whatever, it didn't matter! What mattered was we were going. Not only were we going, we were staying at the hotel where the superstars were staying.

I remember the superstars in my down line. Mister Superstar three levels removed from me came up to me at a meeting once and said, "I've got a good thing going on here. I don't want you to communicate with any of my team, okay?"

Taken aback by his words, I didn't know what to say other than, "Okay."

Our excitement started at the Calgary airport. We recognized a few fellow multi-level marketers on board who were going to the same place we were. Craig and Alesia picked us up at the airport and took us to our hotel, then out for dinner. It had been a year since we had seen one another. I went to the classes I had signed up for. I was pleased that Vince actually attended his classes as well. This time, I did not spend as much money as I had done in the past. We enjoyed getting away from our everyday life and visiting with our American friends for a few days.

Arriving back in Calgary without the cloud nine feeling saddened me. Had I had enough of this rah rah business? I kept going to the weekly meetings to be around the excitement that I did not catch in Dallas. Still not receiving it, I had to find something else to excite me through the winter. I had brought home a sample tape of some famous guy's speech. To my surprise, Vince did not get upset when I asked if I could go to his seminar.

I was off yet to another tax-deductible seminar, this one in Columbus, Ohio. I invited my eldest daughter, Josephine, who had also started her own business with another MLM company, to join me.

We enjoyed learning from those famous speakers, who we had never heard of! It was also a fun weekend away, and we enjoyed talking about what we had learned and how we were going to apply it to our businesses.

The money was really growing because of Mister Superstar on my third level. No, actually it was because we got someone on our first level, who got someone on their first level, who got someone on their first level. That's how multi-level marketing works. You never know, who knows who! It's about getting paid on the efforts of others. That's why you never give up.

Still wanting Vince to be a part of my business life, I said, "Are you sure you do not want to be part of the MLM business? What they have been teaching me is finally happening just for hanging in there. Are you ready to come on board? Look how much our residual income is growing!" I did not give him a chance to talk. "We are missing out on the full pot at the end of the rainbow here, with all your energy going to your business. We should both be doing MLM full time!"

That was a very bold statement on my part, and I had no clue what I was talking about. The only thing I did to make this business successful was bring it to Calgary, and others made it happen. I had put myself in position to reap the rewards.

Vince exploded. "You want me to give up my business of twenty-five years, the one I started myself, to do this MLM stuff? Are you sick in the head or what? I will absolutely not be quitting *my* business to build *your* business, no matter how much money is coming in. Get it?"

What had I been thinking? Of course he would get upset at such a suggestion.

Chapter Twelve

Multi-Level Mail

Do you know why you do the things you do?

I started beating myself up emotionally again. I remember thinking, "I don't know how to run this business. My husband doesn't believe in me, he doesn't want to join me. I'm always on my own!" Perhaps I didn't believe in myself. Was I ever going to get what I wanted? Did I even know what it was that I wanted anymore? There was that undisciplined mind at it again!

I started to wonder why I bothered living. Yes, living, why even bother living? That shocked me. Where did that come from?

I wanted recognition. I wanted to be acknowledged. I wanted some appreciation. I wanted some attention. Having lived the "poor me, nobody loves me" perception of life, I was attracted to the possibility of receiving recognition through this type of business. But I was still not receiving it. The MLM Company only paid attention to the superstars. They were the cause of the company's financial success.

After many requests from the multi-level marketers, the MLM Company announced the launch of a fancy computer program that opened up the possibility of seeing the names and email addresses of all our down lines. It would show us how many customers and business partners each of us had within each level below us. I was quite fascinated as I educated myself with this new system. Then a thought came to me. "I could send everyone an email message!" I typed up my message of encouragement, announcing who I was and how I came to be in their up line. I was ready to click on the send button, but I paused. Mister Superstar had told me once not to contact his team. He said he had been in networking before, and he didn't like it when others butted in on his business.

Oh well. Click!

The next day I checked my emails. Nothing! Didn't anyone care? Care about me? It was because of me that they were in this business!

The next day, I was on the phone when I checked my email. Lo and behold, I had a response! It was a very long, nasty message from Mister Superstar. With one ear paying attention to the conversation on the phone, I skimmed the words on the computer screen. I didn't like what I saw. He asked me who I thought I was, and what I was trying to prove, emailing his team when he had asked me not to. He also accused me of sneaking around on him as he didn't receive the message himself. One of his partners had brought it to his attention. As if it was my fault his email address was incorrect in the system! I immediately deleted the message, and deleted it from my deleted files as well, never to read it again. I was distraught that someone could be so nasty and not even consider the content of the email in the first place. I wasn't butting in; I was just saying hello! But why had I needed to do that? I was not yet ready to face asking myself what need I was filling by wanting to send this email. I did not receive any other replies.

My spirit was crushed. I was not able to attend meetings for a month. I did not know how I could face him, or how I was going to handle the encounter. I knew I had to forgive, and then get the courage to go to a meeting, or I would be an emotional mess.

Eventually, I did forgive him, just enough that I could go back to the meetings, but I kept my distance. I did not go anywhere near him for some time. I continued going to the meetings, most times without bringing a guest, watching these superstars and their prospects interact, and wondering why they were so lucky. I just didn't have what they had to close the deal and persuade someone to join the company and start their own business.

Eventually Mister Superstar came up to me. He said that it was distracting to a team when someone else tries to get involved, and he hoped I understood why he had stood firm in his request. I honestly can't remember what my response was. Inside, I was probably calling him a few colourful names, but didn't have the courage to say them out loud.

Feeling worthless, useless, and not knowing where I belonged, I kept going to the meetings anyway, because I liked the energy, and the money that was coming in.

Vince liked the money, too. He surprised me one night by coming to the meeting. When the meeting was finished and the conversations began, he went up to Mister Superstar and said thank you. Yes. My husband said, "Thank you." Not to me, but to Mister Superstar, a man who recruited more superstars who became 'rookies of the year' winners at the annual conference. And these rookies recruited someone else, who became the 'rookie of year' next year. These young rookies, who had everything I didn't.

I could not believe my ears. I was very upset and deeply hurt by Vince's actions. How come he didn't thank *me*? Why would he thank me anyway? I had turned into an aggressive multi-level marketer. I was the cause of our home being turned upside down. I had still not learned how to communicate or even know what I was trying to communicate.

Then, I had an epiphany. I realized that I was envious and jealous. These superstars were being acknowledged by the company, their peers, and now by my husband. I was blaming and pointing fingers at others, but I needed to take a look at myself. There was nothing *wrong* with these superstars. There was nothing wrong with *me*. I just had to let go. I wondered what they had that I didn't. Why things were going so well for them and not for me. Why I couldn't be popular and successful like them. Was there something missing? If so what was it and when would I discover the missing piece?

Coffee Break Thought

What would my
life look like
if I allowed God
to be the Master
of my Life?

Chapter Thirteen

Multi-Level Makeover

Are you doing the same thing over and over again expecting different results? That's what we call insanity!

I insanely kept speaking up and pretending I was a 'somebody,' somebody important. I was making money now, and I could show my family the money. But they could not have cared less. Was it time for me to get a multi-level makeover? Was there a deeper message in all of this mess? I would soon find out!

I remember wondering why so few were responding to my MLM opportunity. I spontaneously asked God why this was. It's as if they don't trust me, God. The answer came immediately. "Why should they trust you, when you don't trust yourself?" Could that be true?

Driving on the highway towards Black Diamond one day, I got the courage to share my struggle about trust with my MLM friend Terri.

Right away, she said, "Self worth issues. You don't trust yourself, don't believe you are worth being heard, and don't believe what you are sharing about MLM is trustworthy, Dorothy. That is what others will perceive. They can see right through you, girl." Wow, it made perfect sense. Now what?

I had thought Vince was the one with the issues. He felt threatened. I was making money now. He would lose his position in the family. But not so: *I* was the one with the issues. It had something to do with what was missing in my life, and it would take time for me to understand the full picture.

The money had increased each month. That would account for his strange behaviour, I thought. He thought my behaviour was strange, too. Two strange people becoming even stranger. As if our behaviour was not strange enough already! I had joined in, reacting to his criticism and comments at every chance, and had become dissatisfied with how things were turning out.

Vince was satisfied with his life. Why wasn't I satisfied with mine? Why had I bought completely into the MLM teaching of always wanting more? This strange behaviour was infecting our family; would it ever go away? He had watched my excitement level at the meetings. I would nod my head in agreement with what the person at the front of the room was saying. What was happening to me, the one he loved and protected?

How could he continue loving this new woman with

this new attitude? He had become uncomfortable around me while being gently pushed out of his comfort zone. And how could I continue in this relationship as this New Woman with the same Old Caveman, the Citizen-Against-Virtually-Everything Man? Were we both insane?

Yes, insane. That was exactly how I defined myself in my marriage. I was insane, and so very tired of the same results. I was tired of being sad, tired of fighting depression, tired of getting nowhere in my emotional life, and tired of *reacting* to life all the time. I was tired of feeling like my marriage was dead, and tired of not being myself, the woman who God gave the breath of life to. I was tired of being who everyone around me wanted me to be, tired of pretending. I was tired of being afraid to say I was a Christian, tired of being afraid of telling people I loved studying the Bible. The biggest fear I had was being afraid to be myself. It was as though I felt I had to protect others from their feelings. Why? Because I felt I was responsible for their happiness. Now how insane is that?

I remember an Italian friend asking her four-year-old granddaughter what picture of the three the little girl was drawing would be for her. Without any hesitation, the child said, "There isn't one for you, Nonna." The innocence of a child: she spoke the truth without thinking of protecting her beloved Nonna from being disappointed.

When would I let go of thinking I had to protect others from feeling or not feeling something? I was a control freak, and by being that, I was not able to let people be themselves either! Why did I think I was responsible for everyone's happiness? How could this be? I needed to learn to be responsible for *my* feelings and let *others* be responsible for theirs.

I was tired of thinking about how to end my life. I was tired of it all. Could that be why I exploded when I started doing MLM? My being responsible for everyone's happiness was stopping me from being powerful, stopping me from being extraordinary. My being responsible for everyone's happiness was justifying why I would do or not do something, robbing me of living a fulfilled life. I think I wanted others to like me, so I became a people pleaser. How insane was that?

I became aware of something else while doing MLM. I became aware that a lot of people were dead, even though they were breathing and pretending but they sure were not alive! In that way, they were just like me; but so many of us are not willing to look inside to see that we are solely responsible for creating our insane life.

I remember asking why God had brought this MLM business into my life. Did God want to bless me? What was the blessing that I was to receive? I was at the right place at the right time, with the right person to show me the right business, so that I could receive the blessing that had my name on it. God had stirred up my life for sure. Could I be born again for the third time? Was I being told, NOW is the time to 'espress o-u-self,' before it was too late? Was this a spiritual awakening through MLM that God had prepared for me?

I felt so alive and thoughts of celebrating my 50th birthday were swirling around in my head as I wondered how I was going to espress-o myself for my big birthday! I asked Vince, "What are we were going to do to celebrate my birthday?"

He said, "What do you want to do for your birthday?"

"Oh, you know what I would like to do? Go to Hawaii for a month!" I responded.

"You know I can't go for a month, and you know I don't like Hawaii!" he said.

I chose to look into a cruise, so we could both do whatever we wanted. I booked a two-week cruise to the Panama Canal. I started shopping. I would make sure that this would be a time to remember.

I thanked Vince for the opportunity to spend, spend and spend more, for making this possible because of all his hard work and the extra money coming in from the MLM business. I sent a gift card from a local restaurant to each of my MLM customers in honour of my special birthday, thanking them for their support.

I got lots of phone messages, including a call from Italy to wish me a happy birthday. I was so pleased that I was being thought of. My daughters went out of their way to cook a home cooked meal for me, which was what I had dreamed of: them serving me, and I would sit down and do nothing. My friends gave me a special treat, too; lunch out and a day at the spa. Terri and I went to a favourite hangout of hers.

I remember that was our last dinner together. She shared how hard it was to be around friends who didn't want to talk about dying and appreciated my listening ear while she shared her reality.

We flew to Miami, and waited with the crowds of people to get onto a bus to take us to the boat. The people we saw at the airport, it seemed, were all over seventy. Vince looked sad and said to me, "Where are you taking me? What kind of fun are we going to have with all these elderly people?"

I said, "I'm sure there will be other younger people on board."

We went for our first dinner, so pleased to be sitting with three other couples that were a bit younger or a bit older than us. What a relief that was!

I had been thinking of what I would do that was different, for my special birthday. There was no way I was going to let this one fly by without being outrageous. I had a few thoughts up my sleeve. The day before my birthday I decided to take a risk and tell Vince. "You know what dear? I've always wanted to go topless and they have a topless deck on the boat. I'm going to do that for my birthday. The other thing I want to do is smoke a cigarillo."

I could tell by the look on his face that he was thoroughly disgusted, but I was relieved. I had said it, and now he and I would have to deal with it. He said, "What kind of a Christian woman are you, thinking such things? And you quit smoking twenty-seven years ago! I'll not partake in this!"

"Great," I said, "you can't participate anyway. The private topless deck is for women only. I don't need you beside me to smoke, either. It's no problem, dear. I'll do it alone."

He had a hard time swallowing what I had just told him, and could not believe that I would think of such a thing. He went on and on.

I thought, "Who needs this?" I'm not going to spend my special day hanging around someone who puts me down for 'espressing' myself.

I was on the run, once again off in my own little world, having things my way.

I left him alone on my special day. I did what I wanted to do. I got up early and went for a bike ride. I jogged a little on the treadmill and stretched to the sound of music, and then it was off to the shower and sauna in the ladies' room. It had a huge round window looking out to the beautiful blue ocean. I finished the morning with a healthy breakfast on deck 10 by the pool.

It was an **extremely** windy day, so I rethought my plan to go topless. I didn't want to take a chance being blown over as I walked up the lonely staircase to deck 14. The topless idea was off until the next day. My plans were now changed, but I made sure to keep myself busy. I made an appointment for a special hot rock and exfoliating massage. I relaxed in the library. I went for an espresso, and then relaxed some more. I went for lunch at the back of the boat, and suddenly, before I looked around, it was time to get ready for dinner.

Vince and I crossed paths on the way to the martini bar before dinner, to have drinks with our new friends. He grabbed me and said, "Where have you been all day? I've been looking for you!"

"Oh, just out and about, having fun celebrating my birthday," I told him, a little coldly.

We headed off to the table to visit before we went to a separate restaurant, alone, to celebrate. But we didn't talk much There was no need to talk, anyway, as Vince managed to keep the crew entertained in the dining room, as usual. The head waiter was Italian, so they had much to talk about.

I sat there wondering why I even married this man. I didn't need him. I could do it on my own. **He doesn't even get it.** He doesn't understand that I just want to be me without someone harassing me.

We went back to our usual table, where our new friends were waiting for us. We were all there for different reasons. They knew what our reason was and showered me with gifts and songs. I gave everyone a souvenir from Calgary in honour of my special birthday. I was pleased to receive happy birthday songs with an American accent, a British accent and another language, Taiwanese. We had our very own personal opera singer at our table!

After dinner, I went and bought the cigarillos. I invited my American friend to join me. I was very happy to have a partner in crime, but then, surprise, surprise, Vince ended up coming with us as well! He just watched in amazement as we lit up.

The next day, the sun was shining and the wind had calmed down. I made my way to the upper private deck for topless sun bathing. I imagined that it would be full of topless sunbathers from around the world. I would gain their attention by announcing that this was my first time going topless. They were looking at a Canadian, eh! When I reached the top of the stairs, however, there were only two ladies there, basking in the sun. My hopes for a standing ovation were dashed, but I smiled anyway. There had been two, and now there would be three, one from England, one from Belgium, and one from Canada.

I was satisfied. I had done all that I had wanted to do for my special birthday, and to top it off, I had my photo taken, fully clothed, as we were going through the Panama Canal.

What a special time it was and I gave thanks to God for my freedom and for all the possibilities.

Chapter Fourteen

Multi-Level Mix-Up

Is it better to stand for something,
so you won't fall for anything?

I started going to many different networking events, displaying the company's flyers. I was now earning $2,700 dollars a month in residual income. The number of business partners who had come in was just over 1000. Out of those, only 39 were still working the business. I was being paid on 5000 customers. The income was from all the long distance calls that people were making. From all my personal customers, I made a total of $20 a month, and the rest came from all the other business partners' families and friends in North America. It was very exciting.

With the fancy computer program the company had, I was able to look at each level and see how many business partners and customers were signing up, every day if I wanted to! I would know which business partners were doing well and which ones would quit before they even got the suggested twenty customers. It was mind-boggling how this money kept growing.

I had not signed up any new business partners in

over a year. I no longer saw a need to go to the meetings. But I liked being around people, and learning how to promote my business. I had set up my business at community centres, trade shows, women's shows, the university, and at networking clubs. My creative spirit was very happy.

My friend Leslie was concerned for me, though. She saw that running this business had consumed me. She said, "Dorothy, I am in an awesome non-denominational Bible study. It's called Bible Study Fellowship. I think you'd like it. Would you like to come along and see for yourself?"

I thought for a moment. "You know, I've actually been thinking about getting back into Bible study. It seems like one of the things that is missing from my life!"

Leslie was glad to have received such a positive response. She went to the evening class and I went to the day class. It was now possible for me to get some real direction and focus on God's direction for my life.

Vince was concerned as well, but for his part in the business. He said, "When you are making $3,000 a month, I will consider revising my work schedule."

Wow, was I excited to hear that! I said, "Are you really serious, Vince?"

"Yes I am!" he responded. We hugged each other, looking into each other's eyes, excited about all the things we could do together. We were only $300 a month away.

I went to the mailbox the next time a cheque came, and kissed it. Soon I would have my husband all to myself and we could fly away. I remember telling a few of the regular bank tellers at my branch to watch the money grow in my account, because I was going to be a millionaire. I was inspired as I began to voice my desires and let go of my fear, one baby step at a time.

A lot of my money was spent on advertising in magazines and newspapers, as well as slogans on the magnetic signs for the car. I had a lot of fun creating catchy phrases for people to notice. When we went out of town and rented a car, I would be sure to bring the magnetic signs. Everywhere I went, MLM was on my mind. I advanced my advertising ideas and had the car professionally done with advertising on the side windows, thinking people would go to the website just to satisfy their curiosity upon noticing my two happy espresso cups. If they did go to the website, I didn't know about it. They did not call with any questions about the business.

But I was much happier at home now that our arguments had subsided. I started including my family in my life by asking for their help when it came time to set up a display of the company's brochures and flyers. I met many interesting people who had the entrepreneurial spirit, too. They were alive and on fire. They were unstoppable.

I attended many luncheons. I gave my little infomercial with passion and confidence. I would speak from the heart, not the head. I let go of my fear. I made appointments to speak to heads of non-profit organizations, CEOs of small companies, lawyers, and store managers. I would just share my excitement about what MLM could do. It did not matter to me what they said. I filed their business cards carefully in my desk drawer in my office, no matter if their response was positive or negative. I thanked God for the money that was coming from heaven. It no longer bothered me if people chose not to join up with me. I was just out there, having fun, fun and more fun.

I became comfortable being uncomfortable, yet I did not know how to close the deal. I actually would have got a lot of value out of having had a one-on-one business coach, a mentor.

But that would have to wait. Our daughter Josephine was getting married, and there was much planning and work to be done! It was time to start informing our family and friends. For sure we would include Alesia and Craig. They said they would love to come up to Canada again. My spirit was soaring with excitement. My daughter would have the wedding I never had!

I remember the joy in planning a somewhat typical Italian-style bridal shower with all the surprises that I had up my sleeve for everyone to enjoy. It didn't seem to matter how tiring it was, because I had time to do it. That was all I had: time. I didn't have to show the business if I didn't want to; it was growing without my help!

But my spirit was sad during that time, too. I had to say goodbye to my friend Terri after her long battle with cancer. When we met last, I was not able to say 'goodbye,' nor was she. In her hospital room, we just looked each other in the eye and said, "See you later." On her last day, lying in bed at the hospital, she said, "I'm so lucky. Look at all the help I have here. I just have to push a button and someone will come to help me. Even though I'm not able to push it, it's still there."

The next day when I went to see her, she was in a coma. I stood by her side for a few moments, touched her arm, and said, "Follow the light in front of you, Terri. I'll see you again someday."

I went home remembering how we met, how we got to know each other, how she encouraged me to open up to my feelings and talk to a counsellor, how we prayed, how she encouraged me in my business and included me in her internet marketing conference calls with her up line, how we enjoyed walking and talking around her inner city neighbourhood. I remember complaining one day about the ice on the pathway, saying that it wasn't safe for us to walk there in those conditions. She immediately spoke in her usual free way, saying, "What? Do you want the bleeping ducks to come up out of the water and remove the ice?" I smiled and asked her not to swear. She swore five more times, grinned at me, and then we continued our walk on the river path. I remember telling her that I had never met anyone who swore so eloquently. Her words would just flow smoothly out her mouth. She was not afraid to just be herself.

When I told a few MLM friends about Terri's passing,

I learned from them that the MLM Company was reviewing their way of doing business. The company closed the doors to all its independent business owners in the United States. Canadian business owners were put on hold until further review. It was just two weeks before the wedding.

In October 2004, just after Josephine's wedding, I called Alesia and Craig to thank them for coming to the wedding, and also to thank them for taking the time to tell us about this MLM Company back in November 1999. I was sincere in thanking them. MLM woke me up. It enabled me to completely engage and enjoy the wedding. I spoke at the wedding, enjoyed my role as the mother of the bride. I had so much fun helping my daughter, and took every opportunity to share my enthusiasm. Before MLM, I held back on everything. Now, I was unstoppable. I was being me, the one who I was created to be. I was ready and willing to surrender all and open my heart to myself, my God, and my family.

I had welcomed a son-in-law, said goodbye to my daughter, and said my final good bye to my friend Terri. What would my goodbye to MLM be like?

Having found out about the company's situation, I

then discovered that the news had sent the multi-level marketers scurrying off, looking for something else to do. Some of them had heard rumours of a sale and got out early, or put two and two together when the company had merged with a traditional company some two and a half years before. But within the big mess, there was another offer put on the table. I would be guaranteed my income for a year because my renewal fee was up to date. However, I would have to agree to build a business in another industry within the MLM structure.

I didn't understand how this could have happened. I didn't know what to do, but I decided to go with it. What would I do if I were not doing MLM? It was my business, my life. It kept me busy while living with a busy family.

Then the unthinkable happened.

My income started dropping each month. Lots of the independent representatives and business owners below me left the company, and had their family and friends cancel their long distance service.

I stayed on the service, as did my customers. I shared the situation with some of them, asking them to give me a chance to build with a new company. I quickly realized that sharing my feelings about what was going on, in tears, with my customers was not professional. I stopped, and sent a letter of apology to the ones that I had already talked to.

I started scurrying around, trying to store up my little piece of the company. Then I started receiving phone calls from Saskatchewan, Ontario, Victoria, Ohio and Colorado. The calls were from representatives who had gone to other companies before this happened, and from other MLM people I had met. It seemed everyone had heard about what had happened, and were calling to encourage me to join *their* team.

I thanked them for their calls, but made sure they knew I was not interested in taking a look at what they had. I was mad. There was no way I was going to listen to their verbal diarrhea! I was confused enough without listening to them!

As time went by and I calmed down, I organized my time so that I could be on coaching calls once a week with one of the speakers I had met in Ohio. I became motivated and this helped me to see the benefits of joining a networking club. I became more focused, had more fun, and met new people. I spent all that was left in my account to buy all the stuff the company suggested one needed to be successful!

I asked God to show me if I should join this new company or not. I said, "God, if this next person joins this new MLM team of mine, it will be the sign that I should do this business, too." Well, that person did not join, but I went ahead anyway. I was in a state of panic, and close to utter despair.

At the first major event for the new MLM Company in my city, I saw Heather, from my church. I had just met her the week before, when I volunteered for the coffee bar. She took me under her wing, teaching me how to do home parties. Vince was okay with that, because I would be inviting girlfriends over to see the products that I had to sell.

One day, Heather said, "Would you like to come to Edmonton with me next weekend to meet my sponsor?"

"Hey, that would be nice," I replied. Heather's sponsor had been in the business for many years. This would be something different for me.

I mentioned it to Vince, who was okay with it as we were going just for the day. Off we went in her little convertible Mazda Miata. I appreciated meeting her sponsor, but I told them, "The only reason I am doing this business is so I can keep the money coming in from the other business. I'm not going to give it my all like I did before."

I had told them the truth. I didn't care if they liked what they heard or not. I was not going to do what I didn't want to do.

Having let go of my anger, I started having fun preparing for the home parties in this new business. I invited a leader in our community to attend, and sent a press release about the invitation and how I was going to make a difference in our province. The leader's secretary actually called to inform me that he would have to decline the invitation. Wow, someone actually responded! That was kind of... cool!

My friends came to show their support but were not interested in the products. After a few months of parties and not many purchases, my excitement wore off.

One day, I went for a walk with one of my girlfriends in Nose Hill Park. She commented that she was happy that we were still friends, even though she didn't support me in my business. I told her that I wasn't sure I was in the right business, and that my heart's desire was to be a speaker. She bent over in laughter, asking me why I would want to do such a thing!

Then I got an email that another telecommunications company was buying the Canadian part of the previous long distance company. The new company gave a three-month deadline. If I signed an agreement before the deadline, they would accept my position as a multi-level marketer in good standing, and they would start paying me in accordance with their payout structure. What the heck? Emotionally I was confused, and really did not know what to do. My income had gone down to $900 a month and I had only six months to hang on to it. I was not yet successful with the new business I was building and wondered what I should do.

I signed the agreement and let go of the other business. My final cheque of $900 was in June 2005. But I soon realized that I would be getting paid next to nothing, based on how the new company's system was structured. I had had the opportunity to promote myself into six different positions in the original telecom company, where I would receive a larger amount of money each time. I had only made it to the second position, which didn't give me much of a start with this new telecom company.

My first residual check with the new company came three months after I signed the agreement. It was for fifteen dollars. It was six dollars more than my first residual cheque in the year 2000. I looked at that cheque and said to myself, "Dorothy, are you ready to start over?"

Inside I knew the answer, but I was desperate to try one more thing before I acknowledged it. A life coach!

The timing was right. I found myself a life coach, Stéphanie. Vince did not agree. Imagine that!

I knew she would help me decide what to do with my business. On our first meeting, she asked, "Dorothy, what is it you really want, and what would you be doing if you had all the time and money you needed and all the bills were paid?"

My goodness! Those were questions I had heard before! "Stéphanie, I would be writing a book, doing lots of traveling, and building my business, focusing on what paid."

She said, "Let's focus on relationships first, then the business will take care of itself!"

Relationship first, business second: that was an interesting statement. I had a few weeks to think about our conversation. Vince and I were off to Italy.

Chapter Fifteen

Multi-Level Magic

How much time do you spend being upset?

Upon arrival from Italy I had enough time to do the laundry, pay the bills and we were off again. This time, Vince and I were going to Victoria to pick up the keys to our new condo.

There was magic in the air, a dream come true, a home away from home. We had purchased a condo under construction in Victoria, BC, in 2003, and it was finally ready. Nearly two years had passed as we anxiously waited for this magical moment. I would stay for a week by myself and Vince would stay only four days as he had a lot of work to do with having been away for two weeks in Italy. This magic was short lived. Within two days, I was upset. I was more upset than I had been on the cruise. More upset than I had been about the stupid paint colour just before the fire.

Feelings of rejection were rising to the surface when Vince had the nerve to start buying cheap furniture. He didn't even take my ideas or suggestions into consideration! He had a mission to accomplish in four short days, and that was to furnish the condo as quickly and cheaply as possible then get to work back home. Vince went out for a bottle of wine and came back with a sofa. He went out to get some tools and came back with a barbecue. It was as though I did not even exist! I was not part of the picture.

That was it; I had had enough wasting time putting all this cheap furniture together, thinking over and over how we could have had a lot more fun in the bedroom. I gave him the silent treatment and just left. I left on foot, staying away as long as I could, until I had no strength left. I had been talking about running away so I could write a book, but this was not the running away I had in my mind.

When I finally made my way back to the condo, Vince was lying in bed. We tried to talk about what was bothering us. He would not see my side of the story. I would not see his. He slept in the bedroom. I slept in the den.

He left me alone the next day. I suppose it was payback.

We both had another day to do some thinking and some more thinking. I was looking forward to talking about what was in my head, and actually say sorry for running away, thinking we had an hour and a half to talk before he left.

When he arrived back at the condo, he rushed in. It was time for him to leave to catch his flight back to Calgary. We had our times mixed up. He had to leave.

I was so upset. I could not even say goodbye. I just sat there in misery, shocked, wondering what was going on.

I wanted to know the truth, the whole truth and nothing but the truth. I was not able to concentrate on writing anything, especially not a book. I was sad and miserable.

Time for cigarillos and a bottle of rum; that would solve my misery, I thought!

Slowly letting go of the sadness and misery, I began to feel peace while sitting on the balcony, enjoying the lights of Victoria as I drowned my sorrows.

Memories came to me. God was bringing back other events in my life where I was acting childishly and running away from life. I felt so out of control. I did not want to live the rest of my life being upset. Each time there was an upset in our relationship, it would take weeks to get down to the root of the problem, but we were never able to *really* get down to the source of the upset, because the same thing kept happening over and over again. I would blame him and he would blame me. When would this end?

I knew I needed help. I wanted to figure out what was missing. I asked God to help me get down to the bottom of this way of living that was ruining my life as well as Vince's. I woke up in the morning knowing God would help me and I was completely ready to trust in His direction. My inner desire was to discover what it was that upset me so much. If I was not upset about what was going on at that very moment, then something from the past must be upsetting me.

As I waited for God's direction I wondered what it would be like being the woman God had intended me to be, and move on to an amazing extraordinary life with the man that I loved? I never wanted to be a single mother and was not going to let that happen now, after over twenty-five years of being the almost Italian mamma!

On my first official life coaching session, I was sitting in the condo in Victoria by myself. Stéphanie and I were doing the session by phone. She said, "How was your trip to Italy?"

I said, "Honestly, every time I go over there, I feel like my relationships with my sister-in-laws and brother-in-laws are always at the beginning, because I am not able to speak the language fluently. I think in English and translate the Italian. My story always ends up with my own version. I never know if I am right or not. If I truly don't understand I say so. If I can pull it off, I simply join in the conversation by speaking a few simple phrases or respond with the correct emotion. It is quite a game I play."

"How many times do you make up your own story even though you speak the same language?"

"What do you mean?"

"Dorothy, is that how you run your everyday game of life with Vince as well?"

"I don't understand?"

"Well, our lives are as real as our perception," she said. "You perceive that your relationships with your in-laws are always in their infancy. How do you perceive your other relationships, your every-day ones, especially your relationship with Vince?"

"Oh my goodness!" I answered. "Is that why my life

is so emotionally crazy?"

"You tell me, Dorothy," she said.

My story of being rejected by my husband was not real. It was my perception. With that understanding, now what would I do? Could I become aware of this perception in all areas of my life? Was I **now ready** to communicate with myself **clearly**, so that I could communicate with my God, my family, my friends, with my world? Was I?

Stéphanie said, "Dorothy, you would benefit greatly by learning to express yourself. Would you like to be the benefactor of peace?" She insisted that communicating in the language of love, rather than that of anger, would get better results.

Express myself! That's the understatement of the century! Mamma Mia! Express myself! I was afraid to express myself! I seemed to run away when this fear would take over my entire being. Express myself, Mamma Mia! I think this coaching is going to help me. (See page 243 for steps I took 2B me.) Expressing me with my body by running away would soon change, and I was very excited and frightened at the same time.

"Yes, I would like to benefit from peace." Then I asked

her, "Why do I always run away when I am upset?"

She said, "We are to learn a lesson through every experience we have. If we don't learn it, it keeps coming back. And when we run away, we don't learn the lesson."

That statement blew me against the wall oo fast I could hardly breathe. She had made me realize I was sabotaging myself.

Stéphanie was very good at asking questions. She said, "Dorothy, how do you speak to yourself?"

"I don't understand," I said.

"Well, do you speak honestly, gently, and lovingly to yourself?"

I started to cry. It took me a long time to answer her question. Finally, I said, "If I treated my friends the way I treated myself, I would not have any friends. I've always beaten myself up. I've always thought I was not worthy of being loved or being happy. I've always thought I didn't deserve anything good!"

She responded by saying, "I am so happy for you, Dorothy. Now you can move forward in your life. I would like to invite you to start loving yourself, and pay attention to yourself by facing the emotional darkness inside of you."

I was a total wreck. I felt like a rag doll. How could I have learned all these truths in such a short time? Was this the real missing link in my life? Now, I believe it was. I was finally willing to realize that I was *worth being loved.*

She encouraged me to take care of myself by exercising, meditating, eating healthy, drinking lots of pure water, and quieting my mind while enjoying the sights and sounds of nature. "Since you are going to be purifying your body, how about pushing it to the next level and give up sugar and caffeine," she said.

Sugar? Caffeine? I might be able to give up sugar, but caffeine! Are you nuts? As those thoughts were going through my head, I shyly and quietly asked her why.

"So that you can gain clarity while writing your book," she said. (See page 243 for steps I took 2B me.)

As I started putting her suggestions into practice, I asked myself a very important question...

What do

I

really want

for

my life?

Chapter Sixteen

Multi-Level Mould

Are you ready, ready to break out of your mould?

I had walked into MLM knowing I had to break the mould of stay-at-home mom. Maybe it was time to break the mould of multi-level marketer. How about the self worth mould? Was it time for me to get rid of this nagging feeling of being worthless?

I remember very clearly the first time someone said I had issues with self worth. I was on my second visit with a grief counsellor in 1998. She said I had issues with self worth, and I thought *something's wrong here. I came to get help with the loss of my mother. I didn't come here to hear what you just said. And what are you talking about anyway?*

Only I was able to figure it out, in the end. With Stéphanie's help, it would become clear, loud and clear.

One month into the coaching, I asked Stéphanie to be my long distance customer. She said, "Is that what you are passionate about?"

"No, but it is a great way to get the money to do the things I want to do."

"How about getting paid for what you love to do?" she said.

"Get paid for what I love to do?" I questioned. The concept was alien.

"Yes, that's right, Dorothy. What do you love doing?" she asked.

"I am passionate about helping others, about making a difference in the world," I replied. "I made a difference in the world by providing a loving stable environment at home without pay. How am I going to get paid helping others? But I would love to be a speaker. If I could only have the passion of an Italian, then I could be a speaker. I've watched them in action! In everything they do, you see passion. But then who is going to pay me for that, and what the heck am I going to speak about?"

"If you do not allow yourself to be paid for what you love to do, you are no different from anyone who is lost in the doing versus the being," she said.

I tried to justify myself by saying, "You just do not understand the MLM system. It's way different than the J.O.B. (Just-Over-Broke) system. You spend a few years working really hard building a business then reap the harvest, and then you enjoy your life."

I could tell she didn't care what my answer was. Stéphanie simply responded with, "Tell me Dorothy, when are you going to be ready to give your real gift back to the world?" I left that session ready to ask myself some questions.

"What would I love to do?" I had been getting used to being comfortable being uncomfortable for a few years now. I knew I wanted to be a leader, a speaker. I wanted to write a book and have a very exciting marriage. I knew I wanted to be a friend to my adult children, be happy, and be a fun person. I knew I wanted to love myself, and have a clear, disciplined mind. I knew I wanted to change my perception of life, and trust my intuition. I wanted to have a real open honest relationship with all my family and extended family.

I was ready to be thankful for my past and let go of it.

I wanted to totally trust God, and be a blessing to people around me. I wanted to sing and dance as though no one was watching, and to enjoy my life being aware of all the sights and sounds that God had created. I wanted to believe in myself. God believed in me and loved me. My children believed in me. My husband said he believed in me. Could I start believing in me, and even consider getting paid at the same time?

And why was it always about money, anyway?

I remember when the grief counsellor had shown me a $10 bill. "What's it worth?" she asked.

"Ten dollars," I replied.

She stomped on it. "What's it worth?" she asked.

"Ten dollars," I said.

She crumpled it up. "What's it worth?" she asked.

"Ten dollars," I repeated.

She spit on it. "What's it worth?" she asked again.

"Ten dollars," I said, wondering why she was doing this.

"You see, Dorothy, no matter what happens to you in life, your worth never changes. You are an adult now. You can look at life through the eyes of a grown woman, not the eyes of a hurt child."

Knowing my worth never changed, yet thinking and reacting to life each and every day, how would this knowing become real? How would I put a dollar value on speaking to people? Vince had made it clear that everything was about money. Now Stéphanie was telling me it wasn't about money. It was about seeing value in my message.

I believed this MLM business was about money. Without money, life was pretty much limited. I would have to look at my life and what was it worth in dollars! Would I be willing to take a look? But it was something new, and it caused a stirring in my mind as I tried to put a value on the words I would say.

What was my speaking worth? Could I earn money being a speaker? What would I charge while doing this thing that I longed for? Life was really getting uncomfortable. I was not sure if I could handle it.

My undisciplined mind had kept me in darkness for such a long time. I was beginning another transition, developing out of the dark room. This darkness I had been in was like being in a coma. My MLM experience had stirred and opened me up. I was ready for another change.

I remember wondering if I could cope with more change. Better yet, could my *family* cope with more change? We had been through so much already. What new steps would I have to take to break free?

I had been a great follower. How would my life look, thinking of myself as a leader? I had been a leader in the privacy of my own home, raising my family, but out in public? Leaders must talk to themselves in a loving way, picture themselves as a speaker, and believe in themselves. (See page 243 for steps I took 2B me.)

I decided to start enjoying my life, and to write my book. I decided to start looking at my cloudy perception of life. I decided to start clearing my mind, having fun, being happy. I would consider being vulnerable so I could be 'Free 2B Me,' with no holding back.

This sounded pretty scary, but I would have to let go just to let go. I would have to remove myself from the goal, so that I could enjoy the process. I started spending time being still and thinking about the questions I was asking myself.

"Dorothy, what do you like?"

"I like taking pictures. I like one-on-one conversation. I like the thought of being happy. I like organic foods and taking care of my health. Most especially, I like travelling and would like to go away once a month. I like people who are open and honest."

"Dorothy, what don't you like?"

"I don't like phoney people, gossiping, wasting time, being angry, being depressed."

As I was thinking, I was writing down my thoughts

as well. Things started opening up for me when I saw the true picture of my life, face to face. I chose to sign up for a digital camera course at the University, and a laughter class, too. It was different, doing something just for the fun of it.

I really enjoyed looking at myself in a new and exciting way. I enjoyed the homework in my camera class, and enjoyed being around people who laughed for no reason. Doing a homework assignment, I decided to take photos of my collection of espresso cups. When my son, Peter, came home, I showed him what I had done. He said, "Wow, Mom, I'd like to be you for a day. How long did it take you to take all those photos?"

"It took me three hours."

"Wish I had your time on my hands!" he said.

I remembered what the last six years had been like, and knew that God had brought me this far, and was waiting for me to look ahead and be ready to step even further out of my comfort zone. I realized that I had served myself while doing MLM. Now I was coming to realize that God was preparing me for a life of service to Him.

With all this renewal and expansion of my mind and

allowing God to work in my life, I was able to keep still and just enjoy the moment, the moment of now. This paradigm shift in thinking was helping me realize that if God had brought me to and got me through MLM, then everything in my life was there for a purpose. I only had to trust Him and continue to trust Him to enjoy what was happening now.

Chapter Seventeen

Multi-Level Mourning

**Are you ready to change the way you look
at your life? If so, your life will change!**

I started looking at my life with a new purpose. I felt that MLM was not what I was supposed to be doing. God had woken me up, and now it was time to move on. For the first time, I asked God what my talents were and how I could best be used by Him. I truly felt I was being called to step further out of my comfort zone in encouraging others to come out of their comfort zones, too. God gave me the idea to have a toll free hot line for encouragement available twenty-four hours a day in North America. And I did exactly that: 1.877.499.4276.

Three weeks after my one-on-one coaching sessions had started, and four weeks after the big upset in Victoria, I walked into a seminar that I had committed to seven months before. As I listened to the speaker share *...the way this program works...So you can create amazing possibilities in your life...* I just knew I was to be there. I saw God smiling and winking at me with the eyes of my heart. I trusted that God would teach me about my past so that I could look at my future without my past in front of me. I was ready to look deep within and see for myself what was inside.

Remembering my six years as a network marketer, I didn't know that without believing in myself I could do nothing. I had believed in God and accepted his son Jesus Christ early in my marriage. Over and over again, I convinced myself that I could do all things through Christ. But the one thing missing was belief in *me*. I was created in the image of God, and how dare I not believe in myself with the spirit of God in me.

My preconceived idea was that leaders or speakers were perfect. With eyes and ears open I discovered the truth. Leaders and speakers were far from perfect! I became aware that God qualified the called, not called the qualified. Why had I believed a lie for so long? Why had I believed that Christian leaders had to be perfect? With such limited thinking, I was ashamed to say I was a Christian because of not being able to live up to how Christ lived. Now I knew better. Christianity was about *grace* from God and freedom from self. I did not have to pretend anymore, and I could now be a leader, too!

I remembered my strong desire to be just like the Proverbs 31 lady—a leader in her community—so I took a closer look and studied her for the summer. I tried to put her act into my life and gave it up after a couple of weeks, saying to myself, this is too hard. I think **I'll just be me**.

I took on being one of the small-group leaders at that seminar. I thought I could choose to be a leader or not to be one in my real life, as the real me. I would see how I could handle it, then follow the desire of my heart, which was to be a real leader and a 'for real' speaker. I really enjoyed being a small-group leader. I made sure I attended all the meetings and small-group leader conference calls. It worked for me.

Once I gave myself permission to be a speaker, I started planting the seeds. I started asking others if they were looking for a speaker and I was off, onto a new start in my very own business for God, sharing with and encouraging the community, standing up and speaking at every opportunity.

I followed up with nearly everyone I came in contact with at every event. I spoke from the heart and inspired others to be who they were created to be. I was in real conversation everywhere I went – funerals, networking events, family gatherings, and mother/daughter, mother/son, husband/wife conversations. I had gone from protecting everyone, from possibly being upset in the past, to saying what needed to be said right now. It was weird. My voice was now being heard. Although I was not officially a speaker, I was experiencing my voice. I totally came out of the pantry at home to experience being uncomfortable once again, to be used by God. I became aware of what I really wanted to do with my life and what my commitments were.

As I considered letting go of being a multi-level marketer, I knew I would have to call all my customers and inform them of the change. I was given the opportunity when one of them called to ask me about an issue they had with their phone bill. Right then and there, I told my customer what was going on in my life and that I would no longer be their representative. I did a three-way call to help them with customer service. She said she was sorry to see me go, never before experiencing such positively outrageous personal customer service before and wished me luck. Then I proceeded to call them all.

I remember the relief I felt after getting through the whole list. I burned my bridge, and I could no longer go back.

Being committed to being a speaker, I started look-ing into some official training. I got excited when I re-ceived an email for a seminar in Florida on how to be a speaker. But Vince said he could not afford to pay for such a trip. I had also previously asked to go to the ad-vanced seminar of the one I had just completed, and he said he could not pay for that either. My money was gone, but I wanted to continue learning. Suddenly I felt stuck, and I started to struggle again. I was walking up and down the hallway in the comfort of my home, and I could feel panic and fear coming to attack me. My undisci-plined mind was racing. Within minutes I was an emo-tional wreck. I felt I had lost my freedom; there are no words strong enough to explain the desperation I felt. If there had been a gun available, I would have used it right then and there.

I remember wanting to die. I could not live in this entrapment that my life suddenly had become to me. I was crying uncontrollably. Then God brought to my mind questions to ask myself. "What am I feeling? I feel like I am being cornered. When did this feeling first happen? It first happened when I went to testify in court, as a child." That's it, that's all? That was my past! It did not have to go ahead with me into the future. I stopped crying and started laughing. What a discovery! I was free, free at last! What was the rush, I would die someday anyway! I was able to totally let go of the feeling of being cornered.

That's all it takes, really: a desperate moment in time and it's over. My children could have been without their mother, my husband, his wife. I would have robbed myself of the experience of being a grandmother the following week! I was relieved to have become aware of the truth about my situation through my willingness to ask a few simple questions, and to be set free from such terror so quickly. I thanked myself, "Thank you Dorothy." I then began to realize how much time I had wasted with a life of empty, meaningless stories I had created. Now I could live the rest of my life with passion, just like the Italians.

I was ready to let go of the control and submit myself totally to God and what He wanted me to do with my life. I asked myself what my passion in life was. My passion was to have absolutely clear communication with myself and God, myself and family. It now included spending lots of time with my new grandson. My transition from being a stay-at-home mom after twenty-three years to now being a grandmother, 'Nonna Canadaise,' was a long and painful six-year period. When I went to the hospital and saw my first grandchild for the first time, I realized how precious the breath of life was, and I vowed to start, NOW, being thankful for the breath of life that was mine as well.

I had spent most of my life being upset and pushing people away, trying to prove I needed no one. Me, myself, and I could do it on our own. Praise God that finally I accepted the truth; that I can do *nothing* on my own I was given the breath of life to bring glory to God. Now I can live a fulfilled life.

Do you feel something is coming to wake you up from your emotional coma? Remember, you're never too far away from God to come back! God showered His mercy upon me. He saved my marriage because I gave up the desire for power, money, and independence. I got the message loud and clear. I had so much to be thankful for. He taught me these lessons while I was a multi-level marketer. Funny, isn't it? I thought owning my own business would help me cope with my twenty-four hours while my family was busy with their lives. Look what God taught me about me! His purpose was much deeper and meaningful.

Before I started my own business, my story was silent 'Poor Me.' While owning my own MLM business, my story changed to a loud 'Look at Me, I'm Somebody.' Now, living my life on purpose, my story is 'Look at What God Has Done Through Me.' I have learned when to speak up, and when to shut up, most of the time!

Looking back, I had so much to be thankful for. I learned so many valuable lessons while being a Canadian, a girl, a daughter, a grand-daughter, a cousin, a niece, a sister, a friend, a student, a waitress, a secretary, a wife, a mother, a volunteer, a Christian. Looking to the future, I was ready to celebrate being a grandmother, and serve God by answering the calling of Encourager, Speaker, Author. I opened my eyes and looked around; seeing all the people who were struggling, just like me. I was now free to serve my God and share my story with the next generation.

Coffee Break Thought

I am the
Master of my Mind

God is the
Master of my Life

Chapter Eighteen

Multi-Level Mountain

What three things have you failed at while climbing your mountain (your life)?
What lessons did you learn from failing?

I had failed at believing I was worth being loved. I had failed at building my business without belief in myself. I had failed at loving myself and others as we are. But now, I was ready to let go. I threw my failures in the garbage and started looking at what I had learned while climbing my multi-level mountain.

Vince and I became much better friends. We learned to accept each other unconditionally. We let go of the fighting and started seeing each other as human beings created in the image of God. We looked at each other with a much deeper love than we had when we were first physically attracted to each other some twenty-nine years before. In seeing me become a real person, becoming my true self, he became real and true to himself as well. He even signed up for a life-changing seminar in Victoria.

We learned to let go so we could enjoy the next however many years of our lives, fully in love and having fun meeting people on the way. We would walk hand in hand along the ocean pathways in Victoria after I had finished my Bible study and he had finished his run. When a disagreement arose, one of us let go. We would step into the other's world for a moment to see what it was like from the other perspective (sometimes). When anger came into the picture, it lasted a few minutes rather than a few days or weeks. I would acknowledge I was angry, then choose to be happy, or tell Vince I was angry and he would let me vent. Anger became less and less serving to me. He had nothing to prove to me. I had nothing to prove to him. He became a new man. I became a new woman.

I briefly mourned the loss of my old perception of myself and my MLM business, and burned the bridge behind me.

As I came to desire clear communication with myself, I fell in love with me & my life and felt that my love of God, family and self would fully satisfy me. I chose to remove the advertising from our car as a sign to my family that they had their mother back, fully alive and ready to participate in her life as a wife/mother/grandmother. I was now looking at life through the eyes of my heart.

Vince had never liked the idea of having advertising on our car, but I didn't tell him that I removed it, and he didn't notice it as we left to go to the mall that day. When we walked through the parking lot of Market Mall after shopping, Vince saw our car without the advertising. He looked at me and said, "You really love me, don't you?" I just smiled and gave him a hug. I knew that God had everything under control anyway. I didn't have to have it my way.

I let go, as there was no need for me to make a name for myself or an MLM company. I would give all the glory to God while encouraging others. Who knew what the next thirty years would bring us? I was inspired... I was in love...with me, my life, my husband, my God, my family. Because I came to love me as I am and am not, I could love everyone as they were and were not.

Don't you just love happy endings? Wouldn't this story make a great movie? If you think so and you know someone who knows someone who would be inspired to put this story into a movie... pass it on!

If I ended the book there (which is what I had intended to do) that would just be too happy! The truth is... there's more! Vince went to a life-changing seminar and walked out, saying he didn't need any of that brain washing. Not only did he walk out, he walked out after it was too late to get his money back!

I thought he went there for himself, but wasn't ready to look within. I found out later that he went there for me.

We were in Victoria for a week. I had created, in my mind, the possibility of a fun and spontaneous marriage. When I chose to live in that realm, I really had no choice other than being fun and spontaneous.

Being upset with Vince lasted but a moment, and we were off to enjoy the island for the rest of the weekend. We didn't talk. It was silent in the car as we drove down the highway. An hour passed. I saw a road sign for a bird sanctuary and quickly pulled over and turned around. He asked, "Where are you going?"

"We're going to see some birds," I replied.

We had to wait 20 minutes before it opened. We sat in the car in continued silence. I lowered my seat and closed my eyes. Suddenly, I was startled by Vince's voice. "What are you doing?" he asked.

"I'm thinking peaceful thoughts," I whispered.

"Why?"

"So I can have a fun and spontaneous marriage," I said.

"Oh really? And what's your marriage been like the past twenty-nine years?" he inquired.

I just sat there with my eyes closed, then said, "Be still and quiet. Everything is great."

He commented how impressed he was with my new way of dealing with being upset. I smiled inside. He was impressed, but the program was not for him!

Now when he tells me we can't afford something, I just don't believe it. That's what he thinks. I think different. God has lots of money. Me and God, me and money, we have a very good relationship!

Six months later, as I was walking from the car to our church, I saw a penny on the ground, an old, dirty penny. I walked over it. Normally, I would have picked it up and put it in my pocket and said thank you. I stopped. *What's going on here?* I asked myself. I stepped back a few steps, bent down, picked it up, and said thank you to God. As I listened to the sermon, I was overcome with gratitude. God had brought me a long way.

I remember praying, "All that I am, is because of You. All that I am going to be is because of You. All that

I have is Yours."

I put the penny in the offering plate, to Vince's surprise. "Why did you do that? That's an insult to God," he said.

"Obviously you don't know the story of the lady who put in the little that she had. All that I have and am is because of God. He will provide the funds for my book."

I remember being distraught at a time when I wanted to move to Italy for a year, but Vince didn't. We put a plan together of what would have to happen over the next two years, and how much money would have to come in to accomplish such a task. It was a huge amount of money. In my disbelief, not knowing where all this money would come from, I asked for God's help. I wanted so desperately to move to Italy. My grandmother had died, and I wanted to fill my emptiness with love for and from my husband's family. I woke up that Sunday morning with a vision of a lady. I didn't know this lady; I only knew her face. I went to church that day. When the guest musicians started singing, I looked up and there she was, singing a song about being still and knowing and trusting in God. At that moment, I was in tears and knew our plan would work out. We worked very hard for two years, and saved and saved from the overflowing abundance of work that God had provided for us.

Thinking of ways to promote my book, I chose to get new business cards. I had spent a lot of money designing cards or paying someone else to design them. I told Vince what I was up to on our way home from church. I then kept still and silent, and timed him while I listened to his loud complaints about money.

Really, it's not about money. It never is. It's about seeing the value in spending the money. He saw no value in what I wanted to spend money on. Now he was upset again.

"Why do you keep looking at your watch?" he asked.

"I just wanted to see how long it would take you to voice your opinions," I said.

Upon arriving home, I started getting ready to prepare the meal for family, as our children usually came over on Sunday, together. Vince sat down to watch soccer, and fell asleep. I went upstairs to my bedroom.

I could feel my spirit becoming sad. I knew something was up, because my excitement and happiness were slowly departing. I cried for one minute. I prayed for one minute. I took deep breaths for one minute. I created the possibility of being responsible for being happy. I let go of my sadness, while not allowing Vince's opinions to affect me. I envisioned going to networking events displaying my cards, announcing the coming of my first book. Then I fell asleep.

When I woke up, I came downstairs and he was gone! I continued working in the kitchen. There he was, coming in from outside with a smile on his face. "Where did you go, dear?" I asked.

"I went to wash the car for you. Come and see those new tires and the rims, how they shine."

We went outside. "That looks great," I told him.

"You know what?" he said then. "In the real world, you would have to present a business plan and projected costs for this book of yours. Since I'm the one providing the money for this project, I want to see just how much this is costing me, so I can figure out how I am going to get it. We have a lot on the go in the next six months, and I don't know where I'm going to get all this money we need."

What could I say? I just smiled and made an espresso for two, saying "I will have it on your desk in the morning. And don't worry. God's got it all under control!"

All that I am is because of God

Glory to God in the highest

Amen

How about you? Are you ready?

Are you ready to take on your life?

From Me 2 You

Encouragement

Toll-free 24 hours a day in North America

1-877-499-4276

Follow the light and the passion in your life!

Love from,

Dorothy

Afterword

Y ou've been there, and you've seen it with your own eyes. At the company party, there is that woman who is sitting in the chair across from you or at the end of the table. She's either silent and unhappy, or she's on her way to intoxication. Either way, she's making a fool of herself. She's unhappy! You try to ignore her, but she's emotionally removed and won't go away. She's come to the party with her mind full of "he said and she said," or an extremely negative internal dialog of herself that has left her devastated. In reality, it is what he said and what she heard that has thrown her into oblivion with an undisciplined dialog in her mind. That's how she handles herself, and that's why she feels so miserable.

I've come up with a universal phrase, a phrase that anyone can use when they take a stand for themselves. You see, we are being unkind by ignoring what's going on and allowing the negative downward spiral to destroy any of our creative spirits. **The phrase is 'fun goo loo.'**

Have some fun here; make it mean whatever you want it to mean! **Try it on for yourself when your mind has taken you hostage.** Stand up and smack yourself in the forehead with the palm of your left hand and say the phrase loud and clear. "Fun goo loo!"

This can be a fun way of putting a *stop to* the strong attachment that we have with the meaningless conversation that goes on in our mind. Once you learn this fun way of dealing with your mind, you can take responsibility at the party. Don't let your friend or colleague make a fool of themselves. Help them out! Stand up and take them to the loo and ask them what's really going on. Let them share, then do your own 'fun goo loo' song and dance. Don't think it can't happen to you, because it can!

The scene takes place in a hot tub outside on a chilly day. The husband comes home after a long day at work and goes out to relax. She soon follows him with a fresh cup of espresso and jumps in too. He's relaxing; she's thinking 'I just want to have some fun.'

She says, "How about we wear those fun shirts the kids gave us for our 30th anniversary to the Christmas party?"

He says, "That's a business party. It's not appropriate."

She says, "You're no fun, I'll wear mine anyway!"

He says, "If you go wearing that shirt, you can go without me!"

She says, "Why can't business be fun?"

He says, "Those are my business colleagues and I like it just the way it is, and I am fun anyway. I don't need those shirts! I should just put some cement in your mouth!"

As her mind goes over what he just said, he keeps talking. "If you want to wear those shirts to the soccer get-together, we could do that."

She says "Did you say you should put some cement in my mouth?"

He says, "Yes I did."

She jumps out of the hot tub with a disgusted look on her face. She goes upstairs, has a shower, gets dressed, and puts dinner on the table in silence.

When the man comes in, his son says, "What did you do to Mom?"

He says, "Why, what's up?"

"Mom looks pretty upset," the son says.

As she sits there in silence, not answering his questions at dinner, he leaves her alone to be with her miserable self. As the silence and anger continue to stir within her, she says to him a few days later, "I'm not feeling well. I'm not going to the party."

He stays home with her. She informs him that she's not going to the next party either. "You don't deserve to have a beautiful woman sitting beside you at the party." He goes to the party without her. But then she joins him at his company party, sitting there emotionally removed and in silence, wondering why she even bothered.

If only someone had the courage to take her from that table and ask her, "What's going on here? **You're just not yourself.***"* Then maybe things would have been different. **But this doesn't usually happen.**

Can you feel the pain and suffering? Why do we do that to ourselves? Why do we not care enough to help someone out? Why do we run away from those situations?

Praise God those two people have now come to an agreement after one month of being tired of the silence, the anger, the distance and the loss of love. They have made an agreement with each other to take a stand. The stand: love is worth it. Learning to speak open and honestly with each other is worth it.

When they see the other person reacting or getting upset, they are going to ask, "What did you hear me say?" Because with the word 'cement,' she heard him say, "Your opinion is worth nothing. You're not good enough. Nobody wants to have fun with you." What he was actually saying was, "Why don't you just be quiet and give me a moment? I need some relaxation right now after working all day!"

A few days later, after they've spent some time together relaxing away from home, he shares his dream, once again, of owning a convertible. He decides to trade in their vehicle. As she supports him with his dream and gets into the car for a test drive, she's thinking, "This seat is uncomfortable. I don't like it being so low. I hope he's not really going to do this. I'm getting too old for this. I don't like having the sun roof open; how am I going to like having the top down? Blah blah blah."

As she gets ready to say something, her inner voice says, **"It's not about me."** For the first time in her marriage **she doesn't complain, she just says nothing**, and watches him have some fun. So she just enjoys sitting beside him, and he takes her for a ride, after thirty years of marriage, in his almost 'dream-come-true' car. As Vince and Dorothy (yes, it really is us) drive down the streets of Victoria with the top down, they continue holding hands and smile at each other, being thankful for NEVER-ENDING LOVE.

As you learn to be open and honest with yourself and your partner in life, you'll find that for the most part love conquers all, and it never ends. For love is just the beginning, and life is full of new beginnings, every single day!

Always and forever at your service.

Dorothy Sessa/ Mamma D

Freely choosing 2B me... because I CAN

Encourager, Speaker, Author

Epilogue

Wishes

The New Prayer of Serenity

God grant me the serenity
to accept the person
I can not change.

The courage
to change
the person I can.

And the wisdom
to know that it's me!

When you change the way you look at your life... your life changes!

May you be blessed as you let go of the old you, as you gather courage to begin your own business, whether it be MLM or traditional or just begin taking baby steps in discovering who you really are.

May you be blessed in your marriage, in your family, with many authentic real friends! Blessed with peace of mind as you renew your mind and step out in serving your God?

From the top of my head to the bottom of my coffee cup, I am honoured to be a wife/mother/grandmother, and wish to thank my family for always and forever loving *me* as I journeyed to significance, creating the authentic, real, passionate person that I now am, and will always commit to living a fulfilled life, forever growing and learning and failing forward.

Allow me to encourage you, 'The Called.' When your friend calls on you to ask you to help them in their business, remember it's not life and death, it's not surgery, and you don't have to give up your kidney, okay? Let your answer be clear, a simple YES because you want to say yes or a simple NO because you want to say no and live with it, letting go of all the drama and guilt.

Encouragement to Sponsors.... Be the cause of transformation in the lives of your business partners. You don't know how much there is yet to know in a person's life. Read between the lines and help them to move on. Go with them, and be with them on their journey.

Encouragement to New Entrepreneurs.... Give yourself permission to move forward in your life and expand your boundaries. Let go of your fear, learn the lessons, and trust God along the way. Ask for lots of help from God and from your sponsor. Give lots of help, too. If your family or friend says NO, accept it, let go of the 'rejection' feeling. If they say Yes, say Thank You. That way your life is simple. No more struggling.

Encouragement to the founders of the MLM Companies... Your entrepreneurial multi-level marketers are your resource. Your company is only as strong as its weakest link. I suggest you show that you care, by including in their start-up fee a results-oriented education for the human mind so they can fall in love with themselves and their lives. It would be a win-win situation.

Dorothy's Warning Signals

Some warning signals preceding my change were:

- Immense dissatisfaction with my life

- Felt I wanted to make changes in my life

- Becoming aware of what wasn't working in my life, namely anger

- Discovered that I was worthy of love

- Wondered what it would be like to be the real me

- Exhaustion from spending all my energy on trying to please others

- Being tired of pretending

- Increased crying and depression over past regrets

- Realizing that I had had enough of feeling worthless

- Overwhelming desire to 'espress' myself

- Began the frightening process of following the leader within me

- Realized my comfort zone was a dead-end zone

- Realizing I had been blaming others for the choices I had made in my life

- A burning desire to be a whole person

- Speculating about what letting go of fear would be like

- Realizing I had been suppressing my feelings of being cornered

- Daydreamed about being happy

- Being eager to give myself permission to acknowledge all my feelings, both positive and negative

My desire for clear communication with myself created a hunger for change. Once I began changing, courage that had been buried within me surfaced and helped me look at the steps I needed to take 2 really B me.

Me & My Life: Warning Signals

Me & My Life:
Warning Signals

Steps Dorothy Took 2B Dorothy

- Looked into the face of the person who I wanted to communicate with

- Used my courage to say what I meant in a loving, positive way

- Spoke the truth: "Im not OK with what you said"

- Voiced my opinion: "I don't like the way you talk to me"

- Felt the fear and spoke anyway

- Talked to myself in a loving way

- Mentally prepared a positive self image

- Believed in the power of God and that I was created in the image of God

- Asked myself questions (Questions to ask yourself on page 247)

- Did something for myself just because I could

- Took care of my health by a new regime of eating whole foods (not processed foods), drinking pure water, and, once in a while giving my body a break from wheat products, dairy products, corn, sugar, and caffeine, which cleared my mind

- Lived up to my expectations of myself not someone else's expectations of me

- Did something everyday to step out of my comfort zone

- Let go of protecting other peoples' feelings

- The more I got comfortable by being uncomfortable, speaking up and standing up for me & my life – the more I got inspired 2 Just B Me

It wasn't easy, but it was worth it because I gave my life value. As I learned to 'espress' myself I came to realize my opinion was just that, an opinion. It was not right or wrong, it was just an opinion. The more I used my voice and learned to speak out of love, the happier and more statisfied I became with me.

Me & My Life:
Steps 2 Take 2B Me

Me & My Life:
Steps 2 Take 2B Me

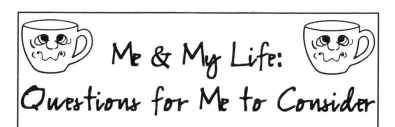

Me & My Life:
Questions for Me to Consider

What do I like about my life?

What don't I like about my life?

What am I willing to change?

What negative thoughts am I willing to let go of?

What am I ready to ask God's help with?

What am I thankful for?

Positive affirmations about me:

Everybody loves _____ **because**

_____ **Loves Herself!**

Appendix

One Liners

Catchy phrases I learned while in MLM

- Mirror, Mirror on the wall, who is the cause of all my problems? Could it be ME?

- Plan ahead. It wasn't raining when Noah built the Ark.

- Teamwork makes the dream work. Plan your work and work your plan.

- Your contact list is your inventory If you edit your list, you edit your success.

- Doubt, fear, ignorance, jealousy will kill your business.

- See it. Believe it. Expect it. Be thankful for it.

- Dead at 20, buried at 80! Whose nightmare are you living?

- God doesn't call the qualified, he qualifies the called.

- Are you working for money or is money working for you?

- If you think you can/can't, you're right!

- I can't show it on the phone, it's 90% visual.

- Success is simple... not easy!

- If you always do what you've always done... you'll always get what you've always had.

- Do today what others won't, so you can have tomorrow what others don't.

- When people give you advice, are they millionaires? If not, do not listen to them!

- People follow successful people.

- Stay away from the 'valley of death.' Tell your prospect you don't have the time right now. Ask for their name and number and tell them you will call them back and explain it. Then call them back. Discipline yourself.

- People are looking for something to believe in.

- MLM will change your life.

- How do you see yourself fitting in? Are you interested in joining me in this business? Can you see any reason why we shouldn't schedule you for training? Do you see a way this can work for you?

- You've got to lie, cheat and steal to make it in this business: You lie in bed at night thinking about your dream. You cheat time out of your busy schedule to build this business. And you steal ideas from everyone!

- Double the belief in yourself. Don't ever sponsor someone who drains you.

- Work on your WHY. The how will come by itself.

- Be – Do – Have, not Have – Do – Be!

- With or without you, I'm going to make it happen!

- Your customers are your strongest resource base: ask for referrals.

- Don't take in the rejection. Say NO to them!

- Start looking for people who are looking for you.

- Prospects are friends you haven't made yet.

- Thoughts – feelings = actions = results.

- Seven days – no complaining – anywhere - - - **miracles will happen**.

- Rich people believe they create their lives. Poor people believe that life happens to them.

- Rich people play the money game to win. Poor

people play the money game not to lose.

- Rich people admire and model rich people. Poor people resent rich people.

- Rich people focus on net worth. Poor people focus on income.

- Play games with your mind, instead of your mind playing games with you.

- Try to see the end from the beginning.

- It's all about attitude.

- Everything that happens to you HELPS, good or bad!

- Let everyone know what you are up to.

- Nothing has meaning except for the meaning you give it!

- Let go of being right (being in control) so you can be rich and happy.

- Anger and resentment is like drinking poison and expecting someone else to die.

- If you're not growing, you're dying.

- Huge goals require you to change.

- Change the imp in impossible to I'm Possible.

- Don't belittle. Be Big.

- Live full. Die empty. Life only cares about results.

- You've got to have coaching because you can't see the picture when you're in the frame.

- Think beyond what is acceptable to others.

- Don't be a volunteer victim. Reinvent yourself.

- Eliminate toxic conversation. Choose carefully who you hang around with.

- Make your move before you're ready.

- Better to be prepared and have nothing happen than have something happen and not be prepared.

- See it. Believe it. Expect it. Be thankful for it.

- You are more powerful than you can imagine.

- Sometimes you have to believe in someone's belief in you before your belief in you kicks in.

- Renew yourself. You can't pull anything out of an empty bag.

- The bottom is overcrowded so reach for the top.

- Help somebody by helping yourself.

- Our brain can be a committee of idiots!

- One minute of anger lowers your immune system. It takes 5 hours to boost it up again.

- You're alive. Live that way!

- You can have everything you want by helping others get what they want. Find something and give it away.

- The poorest of the poor have the money; don't use money as an excuse.

- The definition of a CAVE man: Citizen-Against-Virtually-Everything.

- What's got you turned on? Off? Heart and soul are dead at off, so turn it on!

- Get smart, stay smart. Each of us needs all of us!

- You might as well start with the truth, because you'll end with it!

- You can only go as far as you think you can. You overcome it or it overcomes you.

- Knowledge is experience. Read a book a day!

- Have integrity with yourself.

- Six golden words: Those That Last, End Up First!

- You think the grass is greener on the other side,

until you get the water bill.

- Until you handle it with grace, it will stay in your face.

- When things go wrong, don't go with them. Fear and anxiety = negative emotions = disease.

- If you're going to think anyhow, think BIG!

- Everyone wants it (the lifestyle) but very few are willing to work for it.

- How to stabilize your income in an unstable economy: Talk to Human Beings!

- It's not up to me, baby, it's up to you! I am your ticket.

- It's good that I stopped believing in the lie of the 40/40 plan (40 hours per week/40 years).

- From adversity comes opportunity.

- If we're going to do it, let's do it!

- Profits are better than wages. Profits make you rich.

- I'm busy. Don't flatter yourself. We are all too busy.

- No one can make you feel inferior without your consent.

- We all have the same 24 hours a day.

- I see people busier than me that are working this business.

- Learn one thing everyday.

- Care what you think, not what they think.

- I'm not the answer doctor (don't make their objections valid). Let's get to the heart of the matter: I know you don't trust my company, but do you trust me?

- Keep doing it bad until you get it good.

- Do something. This is the get rich slow scheme.

- R. P. M. Drive & thrive, Power & precision, Passion & momentum.

- This business isn't easy, it's simple.

- I know how you feel. I felt the same way.

- When you are up, the meeting needs you. When you are down, you need the meeting.

- Smile everywhere. People will wonder what you've been up to.

- If you could use my time to free up some of your time, would you get started in this business?

- The only way to avoid criticism is to say, do and become nothing.

What I learned from attending seminars

- What you focus on expands. It's the power of intention, i.e.: Saving your money for a rainy day results in a downpour of rain. Replace this with: Saving your money for an excellent fun day.

- Rich people act in spite of fear. Poor people allow fear to stop them cold.

- Successful people have fear, doubt, and worry. They just don't let it stop them.

- How much money do you spend in a year on the outside of your head compared to the inside of your head? Invest in yourself! Renew your mind, learn about expanding your comfort zone.

- Give yourself permission to invest in yourself.

- Allow you to touch their heart, move and inspire their spirit.

- Most leaders are developed, not born. Good leaders are developed by good people. Good leaders come from being a good follower.

- I CHOOSE TO... I DECIDE TO... Think... Believe... Create... Standing in front of a mirror.

- What do you think about money? What do you think about relationships? What do you think love is? What do you think about becoming a top money earner? Pay attention to what you are thinking. Listen to what you are saying. Watch what you are doing NOW!

- A miracle worker is someone who makes a way out of no way.

- Entrepreneurs are not mentally fit to work for anybody else but themselves.

- Some people are so negative they can walk into a dark room and begin to develop.

- You can't soar with eagles as long as you are pecking around with chickens. Raise your expectations.

Suggestions and questions from counselling

- When I was a child, I felt helpless and unable to stand up for myself because it was dangerous. I am an adult woman now. I have the power to create what I want.

- What new decisions can I make? What will I do that is different?

- What steps have I taken in the last ten years that let people know that I am hurt and angry?

- Give prayers of thanksgiving, and then there is no room for complaining.

- Ask for help on how to fill their needs and my needs... adult to adult!

- How do I speak differently with my children to develop an adult-to-adult relationship, so they know me as a person, not just a mother?

- Why is there a lack of self-confidence and trust in myself?

- What do I feel today? When did I feel this started?

- What three things do I need? What do I need to be doing differently?

- I need to tell people what I need.

- I need to trust my intuition.

- Am I grieving the loss of not having a mother?

- Ask God to reveal what is hurting me.

- What do I need to do to get a life?

- I don't have to be like my mother.

- When I love myself, others benefit from it. I will have gentle conversations with myself. I will allow the victim to be healed. How is this for me?

- Have a letting go party.

Biblical promises that have helped me

- Colossians 2:10 *I am complete in Christ.*

- John 10:10 *I have come that they may have life, and have it to the full.*

- Philippians 1:6 *I am confident that the good work that God has begun in me will be perfected.*

- 2 Timothy 1:7 *I have not been given a spirit of fear but of power, love and a sound mind.*

- Philippians 4:13 *I can do all things through Christ who strengthens me.*

- Psalm 37:4 *Delight yourself in the Lord and he will give you the desire of your heart.*

- Deuteronomy 31:6 *Do not be afraid or terrified because of them, for the Lord your God goes with you; He will never leave you, nor forsake you.*

- 1 Corinthians 2:12 *We have not received the spirit of the world but the Spirit who is from God, that we may understand what God has freely given us.*

Thoughts from extensive Bible Study

- What are some of the things **I am doing** out of fear of what my friends will say? (Things that I do not really want to do.)

- What are some of the things **I am not doing** out of fear of what people will say? (Things that I really want to do.)

- Drifting comes from rationalizing. It appears when I am not anchored. I can trust God. God's dream for your life is so much bigger and greater than you can imagine.

- You can affect future generations by the decisions you make today.

- Be aware of spiritual sluggishness and mental laziness.

- God's word and prayer = spiritual weapons, which destroy strongholds such as thoughts of suicide or ending a marriage.

What I learned from being coached

- Celebrate an accomplishment every day.

- Remove yourself from the outcome; just commit to doing what you know you need to do.

- You know what relationships need mending.

- When you change the way you look at your husband, your husband changes!

- To what degree is this, my story, my story of feeling rejection and loneliness?

- Your pain starts in your head. I create my own story from my own perceptions!!

- Clarify my intentions within all my relationships: what do I really want for my life?

- What patterns do I create?

- I see and understand something in someone else but don't want to see or understand it in me.

- I must communicate with me first.

- Learn the lesson today or it keeps coming back.

- Communicate with love (speak in "I" perspective), not anger ("you make me feel...").

- To what degree am I aware of my actions today?

- When I acknowledge my feelings first, then I can receive healing.

- Love the past; it was a **blessing** to the future.

- I have no control over others' reactions.

- Put my life on hold and heal my most important relationship first.

- I've been trying to be a superwoman on my own, pushing people away.

- Priority is harmony at home. Business will build itself.

- My mind poison stops me from living in peace.

- Start journaling to keep my mind clear.

- Switch panic mode to trusting God.

- If someone does not want to be my friend, send him or her love spiritually anyway!

- I intend to be a beautiful, powerful woman and invite my husband to join me on this journey.

- Because I am allowing my husband to be himself, he is being more open.

- Be authentic. Be vulnerable. Share how the old me used to be and how the new me is now. Be an inspiration.

- Ask permission to follow up when someone gives me a business card. Start a database.

- Come up with a plan, an agreement and commitment to myself. Get clarity.

What to do to be successful in your MLM business

- Make commitment a top priority. Your commitment to God, yourself and your dream will help you through the ups and downs of the business. See the end before the beginning.

- Work your business everyday. When you're up, call your down line. When you're down, call your up line. Have a buddy if you don't have an up line, someone to keep you accountable.

- Believe in yourself.

- Have a vision, and know why you started the business. What was it you wanted that you didn't already have? The how will take care of itself.

- Consistently work smart and keep it simple.

- Develop your own communication skills. You are 100% responsible for the clarity of getting what you want.

- Ask yourself how you can improve your down line?

- Focus on the important not the immediate.

- What you expect is what you will get. You have to change your thinking before you can change your living.

- Communication is number one. Open up the line of communication with God. Then open up the line of communication with yourself. And make God your number one, Make God Your Number One, MAKE GOD YOUR NUMBER ONE.

A quote from Dorothy:
The greatest gift you can give to yourself is: believe you are worth being loved, loved by God and your inner spirit. Then you'll have no other choice other than falling in love with you & your life!

If the Doormat stands up ...
No one can Step on her !

Welcome

Twenty-four things to remember
and one thing never to forget

Your presence is a present to the world.
You're unique and one of a kind.
Your life can be what you want it to be.
Take the days just one at a time.
Count your blessings, not your troubles.
You'll make it through whatever comes along.
Within you are so many answers.
Understand, have courage, be strong.
Don't put limits on yourself.
So many dreams are waiting to be realized.
Decisions are too important to leave to chance.
Reach for your peak, your goal, and your prize
Nothing wastes more energy than worrying.
The longer one carries a problem, the heavier it gets.
Don't take things too seriously.
Live a life of serenity, not a life of regrets.
Remember that a little love goes a long way.
Remember that a lot... goes forever.
Remember that friendship is a wise investment.
Life's treasures are people... together.
Realize that it's never too late.
Do ordinary things in extraordinary ways.
Have health, hope and happiness.
Take the time to wish upon a star.
And don't ever forget...
Even for one day...
How very special you are.

Steps I took in writing Thank You MLM

- Got the idea "I could write a book about my life, it would make a good movie. I'm going to write a book *someday*. Talked, talked and talked about it!"
- I thought I better get busy with this book before the first grandchild comes along. My husband said: Just write the book, would you!
- Wrote my 'Poor Me' to 'Free 2B Me' transition story in two weeks by hand, five days before my grandson was born.
- Asked a friend to read it. She said, "Email me a copy!"
- Rewrote the story as a Microsoft Word document and sent it to my friend. She said this is amazing. You need to give more details about each experience.
- Added more detail, and then gave fictitious names for the characters.
- Gave it to my friend again. She taught me much about grammar.
- Called upon a local speaker, she spent an hour with me over the phone (without charge) as I asked her

lots of questions and told her I'm writing a book about being Free 2B Me. She said nobody will read it. You are unknown! Then she started asking me questions. She said write a book about your MLM experience. I thought that was impossible as I was dying at home alone with a dead MLM business too.

- Found something to be thankful for in my MLM business.
- As I continued writing the book, I told my friends.
- Found a publisher to help me out and started asking questions. (Nothing Happens Without God!)
- Hired a referred editor. She said it's a LOVE story, but was hard to read. Needs to be in first person. I thought: how could she see love in all that pain? (Nothing Happens Without God!)
- Rewrote my story (manuscript) bringing my name and the name of my family into it, which brought more details to my mind.
- Editor said something's missing – dialogue.
- Rewrote the manuscript, adding dialogue.
- Gave the manuscript to my family to read. They didn't like all the details.
- I read the manuscript to my husband.

- Rewrote the manuscript leaving out some details.

- Met with an illustrator who would create the espresso cups from my original photos for the front cover.

- Publisher created the book cover. I gave her great detail and said just do it. She said, "It's your book. What do you want?" She taught me about 'being consistent' with the message in the book, speaking engagements, business cards and advertising.

- Gave the manuscript to my family to read. They liked it somewhat but not comfortable with everyone else finding out the true story about what our family went through while I was in MLM. Melinda said, "Let it sit for two months," to which I replied, "Two months? That's too long!"

- Continued anyway. Struggling, I asked myself, "Why did I come up with such an idea, this is emotionally traumatizing?" Asked God if He wanted me to write this book, then He might consider giving me the title of the book, 'Thank You MLM' came into existence, so I continued.

- Called upon another speaker who shared an hour of his time (without charge) with my husband and

I. He asked me a lot of detailed questions so I could stay focused on my project!

- As I continued I saw another book coming into focus. I called upon God once again. If He wanted me to write another book I needed confirmation for the book title, 'Are You Ready?' came into existence.

- Original editor not able to finish the project. Let it go for two months.

- Called upon a local author who spent an hour with my husband and I. He shared his story on how his book came about. He charged for his time.

- Called several other editors and asked a lot of questions. I wasn't willing at first to follow through with their suggestions. The manuscript sat for another couple of weeks. I then reviewed it and made some grammatical changes.

- I began my marketing strategy. Each time the publisher created what I asked for I got a clearer picture of what was not clear to the public. Many changes were made and the purpose of the book became clear to me.

- I asked the publisher for a mock book so I could pre-sell my book.

- Listened to my husband who kept asking, "Where is the book? Stop selling what you don't have and finish the book."
- Called the publisher for HELP. She suggested an editor, who I encouraged (same as in all my editor interviews) to research my website to get to know me. Sent her the intro and three chapters to see if I liked her style of editing. I did.
- Listened to my friends who kept asking, "How's your book coming along?"
- Started looking for places to sell my book or advertise that my book was on the way! The responses were all positive.
- While I was networking many said, "I'd love to buy your book. Make sure to let me know when it's out!" I could hardly believe what I was hearing. My perception of rejection must have died with the old me.
- Met with my friend and the editor who first worked on my manuscript (the editor who thought it was a love story) to thank them for all they had done for me on my journey to discovering who I was and why I was here!
- I came up with my universal message: Fall in Love

with You & Your Life!

- I finally let go. Let go of being attached to the words on the page. I chose to send the full manuscript. I cried. I clicked on the SEND button and let it go so the editor could chew up and spit out the crystal clear message of inspiration for the reader to understand.
- I approved the editor's changes.
- Talked to two more editors to do a proof read through the manuscript.
- I approved their changes.
- Met with a business coach who I had met at networking events. She asked me a lot of questions and helped me gain clarity on my message as a speaker. She charged a fee for her time. That was the best money I had spent.(Nothing Happens Without God!) She came up with the idea of Thank You Dorothy, which will be used as a website address.
- Met with the business coach again after she read the book. She said something's missing in the message. The reader needs to know what to do next. Next came, the warning signals, the steps and the questions to consider.

- More editing and proof reading was done.

- Inserted the illustration from Ellen Edith who I met in San Francisco. (Nothing Happens Without God!)

- The publisher created a PDF file for me to send to the people I asked to write a testimonial. Testimonials were received.

- My family read the book and gave me their approval.

- I read the book once again. Something was missing, the reader had no contact information to call upon the services of Dorothy the Speaker. ☺

- Inserted a new page for speaking engagements.

- I approved the book. The printers did their job.

- I wrote cheques to pay everyone, with my husband's approval.

- I said: Thank You God, for waking me up.

- I said: Thank You Vincenzo, for your financial support and love!

- Thank You Dorothy, for believing 'Nothing Happens Without God!'

Dorothy's Resources

Bible Study Fellowship

    www.BibleStudyFellowship.com

Landmark Education – Seminars

    www.LandmarkCurriculumForLiving.com

Dr. Susan Janssens, B.Sc.ND

    Maya Health Centre

    www.naturalmoodcure.com www.mayacentre.com

Natalie Gibson

    InnoVisions and Associates – Marketing Specialist

    www.directcci.com

Mandi Crawford

    Roaring Women

    www.RoaringWomen.com

Stéphanie Roh

    Emerge and See Life Coaching

    www.Emerge-and-See.com

Heather Pfeifer

> Amethyst Publishing
>
> www.amethystpublishing.ca

Vanessa Bjerreskov

> Knight Errant Services – Critique/Editing Services
>
> knighterrantservices@telus.net

Cheryl Peddie

> Emerge Creative – Illustration & Graphic Design
>
> www.emergecreative.ca

Anna-Mae Sebastian

> Spirit Seekers Publishing
>
> www.spiritseekerspublishing.com

Pat Kozak

> Freelance Writer/Editor
>
> kozak-lp@allstream.net

Patricia Morgan

> Light Hearted Concepts – Speaker
>
> www.LightHeartedConcepts.com

Eileen Ashmore

> E.M. Ashmore & Associates Inc. – Business Coach
>
> www.Ashmore-Assoc.com

Catharine Haney

>   Katzeye Design – Website Designer
>
>   www.katzeyedesigns.com

Sheelagh Matthews

>   The Idea Garden
>
>   www.ideagarden.net

Ellen Edith

>   Designer of funny cartoons about women
>
>   www.ellenedith.com

PoGoPix Studios

>   www.pogopixstudios.com

*"The average human
looks without seeing, listens without
hearing, touches without feeling, eats
without tasting, moves without physical
awareness, inhales without awareness
of odour or fragrance,
and talks without thinking."*
Leonardo da Vinci

Who are you?
Are you ready?
Ready to be who God created you to be?

Help is on the way...
Stay tuned for my next book:
Are You Ready?

Are you ready to fall in love with
you and your life? Yes, you say.
Well then, let's get started!
Let your life begin...
begin with God,
now that you are ready!

Are You Ready to Consider:

Waking Up?
Falling in Love with You & Your Life?
Just Being Yourself?
Believing it's your Turn?
New possibilities?
Letting Go?
Dreaming?
Having Fun?

Then Ask Yourself

What will happen if I don't:

- wake up?
- fall in love with me & my life?
- be myself?
- believe it's my turn?
- consider new possibilities?
- let go?
- dream?
- have some fun?

For an inspiring talk

about life changes call Dorothy
as your next speaker

Dorothy Sessa

1.877.304.6860